EXECUTIVE EDITOR
Natalie Earnheart

CREATIVE TEAM
Jenny Doan, Natalie Earnheart, Christine Ricks,
Tyler MacBeth, Mike Brunner, Lauren Dorton,
Jennifer Dowling, Dustin Weant, Jessica Toye,
Kimberly Forman, Denise Lane, Grant Flook

EDITORS & COPYWRITERS
Nichole Spravzoff, Camille Maddox,
Annie Gailbraith, David Litherland,
Julie Barber-Arutyunyan, Hillary Doan Sperry,
Lora Kroush

SEWIST TEAM
Jenny Doan, Natalie Earnheart, Courtenay Hughes,
Carol Henderson, Cassandra Ratliff,
Janice Richardson

PRINTING COORDINATOR
Rob Stoebener

PRINTING SERVICES
Walsworth Print Group
803 South Missouri
Marceline, MO 64658

LOCATIONS
Brian and Rosemary Lucas, Catawba Vineyards,
 Breckenridge, MO
Cherry Hill, Hamilton, MO

CONTACT US
Missouri Star Quilt Company
114 N Davis
Hamilton, MO 64644
888-571-1122
info@missouriquiltco.com

BLOCK Idea Book™ Volume 8 Issue 5 ©2021.
All Rights Reserved by Missouri Star Quilt
Company. Reproduction in whole or in part in
any language without written permission from
Missouri Star Quilt Company or BLOCK Idea Book
is prohibited. No one may copy, reprint,
or distribute any of the patterns or materials
in this magazine for commercial use without
written permission of Missouri Star Quilt Company.
Anything you make using our patterns or ideas,
it's yours!

6
GENERATIONAL QUILTING
Who taught you to quilt? Whether a love of quilting began with you or began with your ancestors, you can always be the first link in a long line of quilters.

32
INHERITED QUILT BLOCKS
There are so many projects that can be created from leftover quilt blocks and tops. Let's dive in and take them from extra to extraordinary!

12
STREAMER QAYG LAP QUILT
Create a fast, fun quilt that's sure to brighten up the nursery. This simple striped design is created with the quilt as you go method, which means when you're done sewing, that's it!

38
PLAYGROUND
This playful quilt block is a combination of simple snowballed blocks and flying geese, but the result is absolutely stunning.

18
SEEING DOUBLE
Two stars are better than one and this is a classic Missouri Star quilt times two! Nestled inside the larger star is a mini star. How cute!

46
PINWHEEL FROLIC
These pinwheel blocks are even more fun when you add a plus sign right in the middle. It'll start you on a quilting spree you won't want to stop!

26
SUPERNOVA
When a star explodes it's called a supernova and this spectacular quilt takes the classic Missouri Star block and shatters the pieces across the entire quilt.

52
GOOSE TRACKS
This classic patchwork quilt is different from all the others in one sweet and silly way. It looks like a goose got loose and made tracks across the pattern!

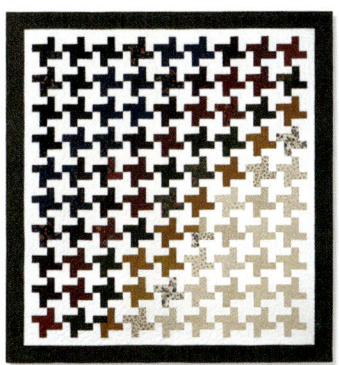

58
BREEZY WINDMILLS
Like the many-colored tulips of Holland, this beautiful Breezy Windmills quilt is filled with the spirit of springtime. Aligned in a spectrum of cascading hues, it's pleasing to the eye.

76
JENNY'S JOURNAL
Find out what Jenny's been creating in her very own studio lately. You'll adore this groovy peace sign quilt and a lovely pine tree quilt in cool, wintry colors.

64
TALAVERA TILE SEW-ALONG
Keep stitching along with us to complete the outer border of this gorgeous quilt with two key blocks: The Super Easy Hourglass and Pinwheel Party!

78
MINI MISSOURI STAR
Totally cute, this mini Missouri Star quilt is a company favorite for a reason! Now you can create your own smaller version of the classic Missouri Star.

66
BOUND IN SECRETS AND LIES
The Quilt Town, USA, mystery continues with a few crucial clues. Read along and watch how Jenny gets even closer to cracking the case!

84
HANDY DANDY
Looking for a quicker way to create half-square triangles? Try our handy dandy strip method! It's a blast to create these beautiful quilt blocks.

70
CHOOSING COLOR
As you work with color, here are a few considerations to help you explore greater possibilities. Learning to use color wisely is a skill that anyone can obtain.

92
RADIANT REINDEER WALL HANGING
Create a holiday wall hanging featuring Santa's favorite helpers! These darling reindeer are here to make the season even brighter.

A note from Jenny

Dear Quilters,

What thoughts enter your mind as soon as you awake? Beginning each morning with positive intentions shifts the entire course of my day. And if I start enough days this way, it changes the course of my week, my month, and my year. It is empowering to realize that our thoughts influence our feelings and, ultimately, our actions! I know that I can choose to focus on positive thoughts or negative thoughts. That power lies within me. So, what does this have to do with quilting? Everything!

The power lies in us to choose our mindset and the ripples of that choice flow outward. For example, if you decide to finally tackle that beautiful, challenging quilt, even though you initially wondered if it was possible, you have triumphed! If we choose to learn instead of leaning away from challenges, we will always continue to grow. And that doesn't just apply to quilting. That mindset is reflected in the lives we lead.

Challenges aren't just found in quilting, of course. Ripping seams, running out of bobbin thread, and pesky tension issues are the least of our worries. Life's challenges are far greater, but we can choose to approach them as opportunities to learn. With every tough decision, we become stronger. With every loss, love can increase. As I ponder the connections that we have with each other as quilters, I am humbled. I know that many of us turn to this artform as a means of overcoming personal challenges. Quilting is so much more than piecing fabric together. We continue to learn and grow with every stitch.

JENNY DOAN
MISSOURI STAR QUILT CO.

GET YOUR
DIGITAL ISSUE TODAY!

Did you know that with every issue of BLOCK, you also get a FREE digital copy online with exclusive bonus content? Access it in your Missouri Star account **RIGHT NOW!**

Quilting through the Generations

For many, sewing is a skill passed down through the generations. Many of you were lucky enough to have a love of quilting instilled in you from a young age. I wasn't one of those people. Although my grandmother did beautiful embroidery and I grew up sewing clothing, I didn't fall in love with quilting until later on in my life. I had been sewing clothing for my family and for the theater, but I didn't actually learn to quilt until I moved to Missouri and took a class at the nearby Vo-tech school. I wasn't sure quilting was something I could do, but I was curious.

"Who taught you to quilt? Was it a family member? A friend? A teacher? Or were you self-taught? Where did that desire to quilt come from? Identifying the roots of your creativity can have long-reaching effects."

During that class I made one log cabin quilt after another. I felt the joy that comes from discovering new variations on quilt patterns and that joy has remained with me to this very day. Despite not having a love of quilting passed down from previous generations to myself, I am grateful to see that my love of quilting has been passed down to my children and even my grandchildren. It absolutely thrills me to see what they create.

Whether a love of quilting began with you or began with your ancestors, you can always be the first link in a long line of quilters. I am always impressed with people who see something that inspires them and causes them to want to express their creativity. Quilters who are just starting out almost always have a tendency to take on a project that's challenging, but it's incredible what people can create when they have no idea of their own limitations. They simply believe they can do it, so they do.

So, my question is, who taught you to quilt? Was it a family member? A friend? A teacher? Or were you self-taught? Where did that desire to quilt come from? Identifying the roots of your creativity can have long-reaching effects. For me, I feel a wave of gratitude wash over me when I consider that quilting has led me to helping my local community, benefiting my family, and connecting with a global community of quilters. It has filled my life with even greater purpose and gives me a sense of belonging. When you become a part of the quilting family, suddenly, you have friends all over the world.

"My mother-in-law taught me when I was expecting my first child and wanted to make a quilt for the nursery. We wanted to be surprised with what we were having, so I used the same pattern and made a girl version and boy version. We had a girl first, but I used the boy quilt a few years later when my oldest son came along!"
◀ —*Kimberly Forman*

"I joined a quilt club. The ladies taught me and said, 'Don't give up, just keep coming back.'"
—*Jerry Marie Poole*

"I started quilting knowing only quilts I had seen in about 1975. No social media. I didn't know there was a right or wrong way. I just learned as I went machine piecing and tying. Then I found Nancy Zieman on PBS teaching sewing and a little quilting. Saw a quilt magazine and on I went. I still don't believe there is a right or wrong way!" —*Ann Papp*

We asked you who taught you how to quilt and here's what you said:

"Seriously Jenny taught me! I'd watch a youtube tutorial and then sew. I literally had no idea what I was doing but if Jenny showed me, I could do it." —*Laura Simms Sandstedt*

"I taught myself to quilt. I have been sewing for years and always wanted to learn and thought how hard could it be? I love puzzles. I can read a pattern and there's always a seam ripper handy if I need it, so here I am quilting 35 years later and loving it." —*Lorri Goode*

"I watched MSQC videos. I had never sewn before and couldn't even thread a machine. One of my son's friends showed me how. I would watch Jenny's video, pause it, do the steps she had done, and restart the video for the next step. I would rewind to do the next block. I am 100% Jenny taught!"
—*Christina Cruse*

"I learned basic sewing skills in high school Home Economics. I liked sewing and was good at it so I continued to sew through my adult life. Sometime around age 55 I started quilting."
—*Margaret Martin*

"My mom and grandmother both quilted. I attribute my desire to learn to quilt to them. My first quilt was an unfinished improved nine-patch that my mother handed down to me from my grandmother. She had all the nine-patches made but got frustrated with the curves of the quilt when trying to piece them together. Not having any quilting experience and minimal sewing experience I decided to sew the blocks to squares. A couple of years later I took the very first Missouri Star class offered. That was almost 13 years ago. I have been quilting ever since." —*Carol Henderson* ▶

"A lady I went to church with who is from England taught me. She's a purist who tears fabric, hand pieces, and hand quilts. I've come a long way baby! I love all hand work and even hand quilting and thought I'd never machine quilt but then we had 10 grandkids and I've stepped it way up and made lots of quilts. And. I. DO. NOT. TEAR. MY. FABRIC!"
—*Linda McMillan*

"My dad taught me how to sew. I was a sailmaker's daughter. I hated sewing until I took on the challenge at 75 to become a quilter. Never been happier." —*Martha Youstra*

"My mom was a master! But she did most of her sewing long before I gained the interest. I started to sew during Covid to make masks. As the need disappeared, I started to shift the sewing to quilts. I wish my mom was still alive to see me follow in her footsteps."
—*Gail Meddows Edwards*

Creating a New Generation of Quilters

Nowadays, quilting and sewing skills aren't being passed on as often to the next generation. There's the convenience factor, sewing isn't a necessary lifeskill anymore, it's less cost-effective to create your own clothing and bedding, and we're all so busy. But taking the time to slow down and share your love of quilting with the next generation can have far-reaching effects. Here are some simple ways to inspire others to appreciate the art of quilt making and have a desire to learn more.

Label Your Quilts
Never be too modest to claim your work and express the effort that went into creating a quilt. Sometimes when you give a quilt away, others will see it and wonder who made it. Don't leave them wondering! Label your quilt as a record of who created it and you may have inquiries in the future from those who want to learn more about quilting.

Create Quilting Traditions
Special occasions are the perfect time to create a tradition around quilting. Why not involve family members in creating an advent calendar or custom stockings for Christmas? Or have them sign quilt squares for a family signature quilt. One quilter had family members sign the tablecloth at Thanksgiving and then she embroidered their names into the cloth. And there's always baby blankets, birthday quilts, wedding quilts, and so much more. Creating quilts to mark special occasions associates warm memories with quilting.

Identify Individual Talents
Do you have a family member with an eye for design? Or one gifted with a sharp mind for math? Involve your friends and family in your quilt projects. Have them weigh in on your color choices, layout, and design. Ask for help crunching numbers. You never know what might spark an interest.

Take a Class Together
Build yourself a quilting buddy in the family by taking someone along to a beginner quilting class. They're so much fun and it immediately gets them involved. That way, if you know you're not the most ideal quilting teacher, they can get an idea for how to begin and you can enjoy the process of quilting together.

Give Back with Quilting
Another way to help others gain an appreciation for quilting is getting them involved with charity projects. Have them help you pick out fabrics for a charity quilt or finish it up. And most importantly, have them involved in the process of giving that quilt away and seeing the impact it has on someone else. Quilting really can communicate love in such incredible ways.

Visit a Museum or Quilt Show
Seeing the sheer amount of possibilities for quilt designs that are out there is often enough to jumpstart a desire to learn more about quilting. They'll learn that it's so much more than a blanket. Quilting is an artform!

Teach the Process
If you have a friend or family member who is interested in quilting, start with the basics and take them to look at fabrics! That's the quickest way to get someone hooked. All those gorgeous fabrics lead to ideas and from there you can help guide them to a project that's perfect for their skill level.

A Slice of Life
Streamer Quilt As You Go Crib Quilt
with Laura Piland

Laura Piland began sewing at the early age of 7. She created a tank top and a pair of shorts for a 4-H project. The only problem was, she hated it. The process was long and frustrating for her and she wasn't satisfied with the final product. The clothes were stiff and uncomfortable, nothing like the soft, stretchy clothes she could get at the store. And so, she swore off sewing forever. Or so she thought.

Just over ten years ago, a friend of Laura's had a baby and she felt the need to make a quilt. The inkling came to her from out of nowhere and she set to work. But she soon realized that the hand-me-down sewing machine she had inherited from her mother wasn't going to cut it. She set out to do some research and bought herself a vintage Bernina Record 930, a sturdy, reliable machine to get the job done! Right away she had plenty of questions. She called her mother, searched for answers online, and watched YouTube videos. Her first quilt turned out to her liking and the rest is history!

Quilting runs in the family and both of Laura's grandmothers quilt as well as Laura's mother. Her maternal great-grandfather was even a Singer sewing machine repairman! Her grandmothers prefer to quilt the old fashioned way, by hand, and her mother likes to piece and quilt by machine, adding the binding by hand. But Laura is all about her sewing machine. As she says, "If it can't be done by machine, it most likely won't get done!" She sews on a Juki TL-2010Q and an Innova longarm.

As a work-at-home mom, Laura is busy homeschooling her three boys, but she makes time to quilt. She explains, "Quilting is to me what fishing is to my husband. It keeps me sane. I also love creating a tangible thing that will provide joy and warmth to others. Most work as a mother and teacher is intangible, so I like that quilting results in something to show for the work put in."

Laura has a talent for creating eclectic quilts and rarely makes the same quilt twice. Her expressive style ranges from modern to traditional and everything in between. She makes large quilts, mini quilts, and any size that suits the project. Occasionally she'll sew other items, but most often she prefers to quilt. And this girl makes plenty of quilts, about 50 a year!

Her business, Slice of Pi Quilts, began in 2016 after many requests for patterns for the quilts she was creating. All of her patterns are available in her Etsy shop. She also travels near and far to quilt shops and guilds to teach and present trunk shows of her beautiful quilts.

READ MORE IN YOUR DIGITAL ISSUE

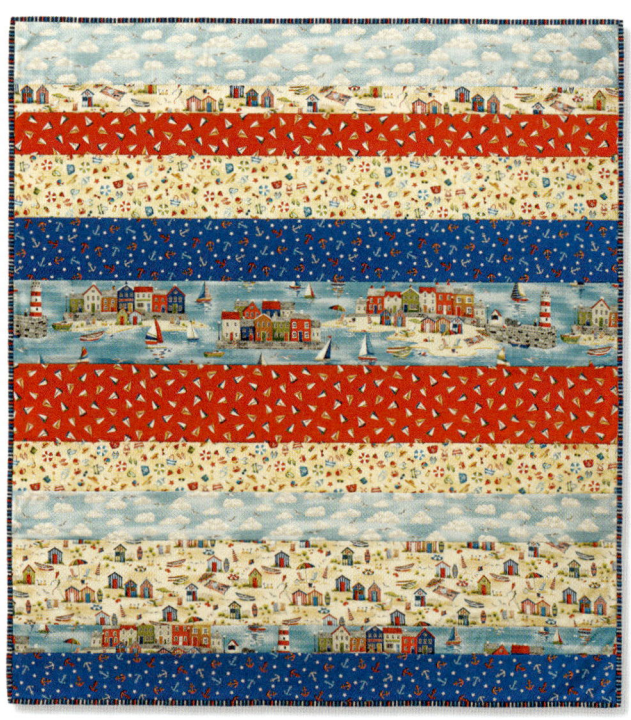

materials

QUILT SIZE
42½" x 48½"

QUILT TOP
½ yard each of 6 different prints

BINDING
½ yard*

BACKING
1¾ yards

OTHER
Missouri Star Quilter's Best Blend Crib Batting (45" x 60")

__Note:__ If you plan to use binding fabric that has a pattern along the length of the fabric, ¾ - 1 yard may be needed.

SAMPLE QUILT
Beside the Sea by Makower UK for Andover Fabrics

3A

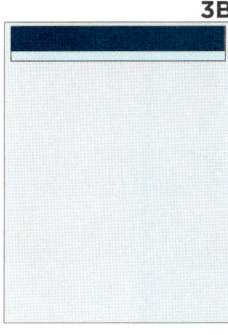

3B

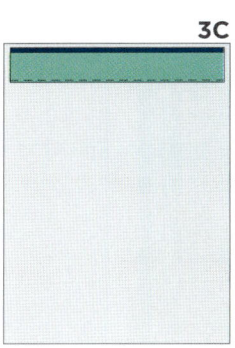

3C

1 cut

Note: Determine which of your fabrics are A-F and cut the strip sizes listed below.

From Fabric A, cut (1) 5" and (1) 4" strip across the width of the fabric.

From Fabric B, cut (1) 5" and (1) 4" strip across the width of the fabric.

From Fabric C, cut (1) 6" and (1) 3½" strip across the width of the fabric.

From Fabric D, cut (1) 6½" and (1) 2½" strip across the width of the fabric.

From Fabric E, cut (1) 5" and (1) 4" strip across the width of the fabric.

From Fabric F, cut (1) 6½" and (1) 2½" strip across the width of the fabric.

Trim all of the strips to 43" long if needed.

2 prepare backing & batting

Place the batting on a flat surface, wrong side up. Center the backing on top, right side up. Working from the center and moving out to the edges, baste the 2 layers together using the free fuse powder.

3 sew the strips

Flip the fused batting/backing over. Place 1 fabric strip on top of the batting, 1" below and parallel to the top edge of the batting.

Lay a second strip on top of the first, right sides together, aligning the bottom edges of the strips. Sew the 2 strips together along the bottom edge using ¼" seam allowance and pin as needed. Sew through all of the layers. Start and stop sewing beyond the edges of the strips. **3A**

1. Lay a second strip on top of the first, right sides together, aligning the bottom edges of the strips. Sew the 2 strips together along the bottom edge using ¼" seam allowance and pin as needed. Sew through all of the layers. Start and stop sewing beyond the edges of the strips.

2. Press the top strip over the seam.

3. Lay a third strip on top of the second, right sides together, aligning the bottom edge. Sew along the bottom edge.

4. Press the top strip over the seam.

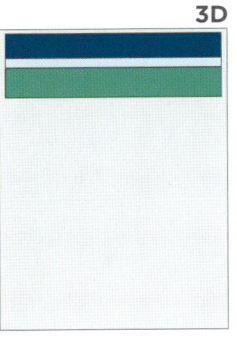

Tip: A walking foot makes quilt as you go so easy!

Press the top strip over the seam. **3B**

Lay a third strip on top of the second, right sides together, aligning the bottom edge. Repeat the steps to add the strip to your quilt. **3C 3D**

Add the remaining strips in the same way and press each strip over the seam as you go. **3E**

4 bind

With the quilt as you go method, the backing, batting, and quilt top are already quilted together. You can add more quilting if desired.

After the quilting is complete, finish your quilt with binding. You can cut 5 regular binding strips across the width of the fabric, then see Construction Basics (pg. 118) to finish your quilt. If you choose to cut the binding from fabric that has a pattern along the length of the fabric, cut enough strips along the **length** to equal 202". You may need to join these strips with straight seams instead of using the plus method, then refer to Construction Basics (pg. 118) for the remaining binding directions.

History of the Missouri Star Block
Seeing Double Quilt

Every state in America has a star on our flag: from the original 13 colonies-turned-states, to the most recent additions of Alaska and Hawaii in the 1950s, each and every one gets a white star on that navy blue field. But did you know that many of them also have a quilting star? There's the Ohio Star, Kentucky Star, and even a California Star quilt block! But today, we're going to talk about the most famous and important star quilt block, the Missouri Star (of course, we may be a little biased!) and what it means to us here at the Missouri Star Quilt Company.

What is the Missouri Star? While little is known for certain, the quilt block dates back to at least the middle of the 19th century, most likely originating in or around Missouri. It is a simple yet elegant block; sixteen quarter-square triangles surround a large square with a diamond in the center. These simple shapes merge into the eponymous 8-pointed star we all know and love!

When we started our company in an old brick building in Hamilton, Missouri, we knew we needed a name that would resonate with quilters. It needed to be something that spoke to our love of quilting as well as our adopted hometown and state. It wasn't long before we settled on Missouri Star; every quilter worth their salt would recognize it, and it symbolized our symbolized our love for the Show-Me State. Plus, Jenny has always loved star blocks, so it was only natural to pick one as our logo! With that, we started out with our single longarm quilting machine, a name, and a dream.

Little did we know that, no more than a decade later, almost every building on the main street of Hamilton would be festooned with that famous quilt block, and Missouri Star would become a household name for quilters across the nation, and even the globe! We've got sewing machines galore, a whole fleet of quilters working together, and Jenny is a full-fledged sew-lebrity. We've designed dozens of twists on the Missouri Star design, and our tutorials about it are some of our most popular online.

Because of the hard work we've done, our ever-growing passion for quilting, and the friends and coworkers we've met along the way, the Missouri Star means a lot to us. It symbolizes 13 years of work, fun, and an uncountable number of quilts! It stands for both the place in the world and the place in our hearts where quilting lives.

In the end, though, what a quilt block symbolizes is really up to you! Half of the beauty of art and creativity is learning what others think about its meaning. Write to us at blockstories@missouriquiltco.com or on social media with stories of what the Missouri Star (or any special quilt block) means for you and yours.

materials

QUILT SIZE
59" x 75"

BLOCK SIZE
16½" unfinished, 16" finished

QUILT TOP
1 package of 10" print squares
3 yards of background fabric

BORDER
1¼ yards

BINDING
¾ yard

BACKING
3¾ yards - horizontal seam(s)

OTHER
Clearly Perfect Slotted Trimmer A - optional

SAMPLE QUILT
Jungle Paradise by Stacy Iest Hsu for Moda Fabrics

2A

1 sort & cut

From the 10" print squares:
- Cut 9 squares in half horizontally and vertically to create (36) 5" print squares. Trim 12 squares to 4½". Set aside a **total of (12)** 4½" squares for section 2 and a **total of (24)** 5" print squares for section 3.

- Set (24) 10" squares aside for section 4.

- Set (9) 10" squares aside for another project.

From the background fabric:
- Cut (8) 6" strips across the width of the fabric. Subcut a **total of (48)** 6" squares for section 4.

- Cut (6) 4½" strips across the width of the fabric. Subcut a **total of (48)** 4½" squares for section 4.

- Cut (4) 3" strips across the width of the fabric. Subcut a **total of (48)** 3" squares for section 3.

- Cut (6) 2½" strips across the width of the fabric. Subcut a **total of (96)** 2½" squares. Set aside 48 squares for section 2 and 48 squares for section 3.

2 make the center squares

Mark a diagonal line corner to corner on the reverse side of (48) 2½" background squares. **2A**

Lay a marked square on 2 opposite corners of a 4½" print square as shown, right sides together. Sew along the marked lines, then trim the excess fabric ¼" away from the seam. **2B**

Press each snowballed corner over the seam. **2C**

Repeat to snowball the 2 remaining corners using 2 marked background squares. Square to 4½" if needed. **Make 12** center squares and set them aside for the moment. **2D**

3 make the small Missouri Stars

Lay 2 unmatching 5" print squares 1 atop of the other, right sides facing. Sew around the perimeter. Cut the sewn squares twice diagonally. Open to reveal 4 half-square triangles. Press. Do not trim. **3A**

Draw a line from corner to corner once on the diagonal on the reverse side of each 3" background square. **3B**

2B

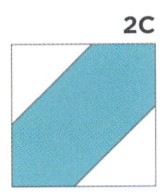

2C

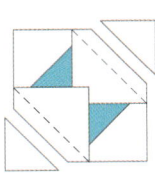

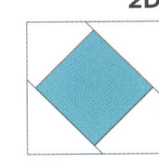

2D

1. Lay a marked square on 2 opposite corners of a 4½" print square. Sew along the marked lines, then trim the excess fabric ¼" away from the seam. Press. Repeat to snowball the 2 remaining corners.

2. Lay 2 unmatching 5" print squares right sides facing. Sew around the perimeter. Cut the sewn squares twice diagonally. Open to reveal 4 half-square triangles. Press. Do not trim.

3. Lay a marked background square atop a half-square triangle with the drawn line crossing over the seam of the half-square triangle. Sew ¼" away from the drawn line on both sides. Cut on the drawn line. Trim to 2½" square.

4. Arrange and sew (4) 2½" background squares, 4 star leg units, and a center square as shown together in rows. Press towards the squares. Nest the seams and sew the rows together. Press.

5. Repeat the instructions to make large half-square triangles from unmatching 10" print squares. Repeat the instructions to make large quarter-square triangles using the 6" background squares. Trim to 4½".

6. Arrange and sew (4) 4½" background squares, 4 large star leg units, and a small Missouri star in rows. Press. Nest the seams and sew the rows together. Press.

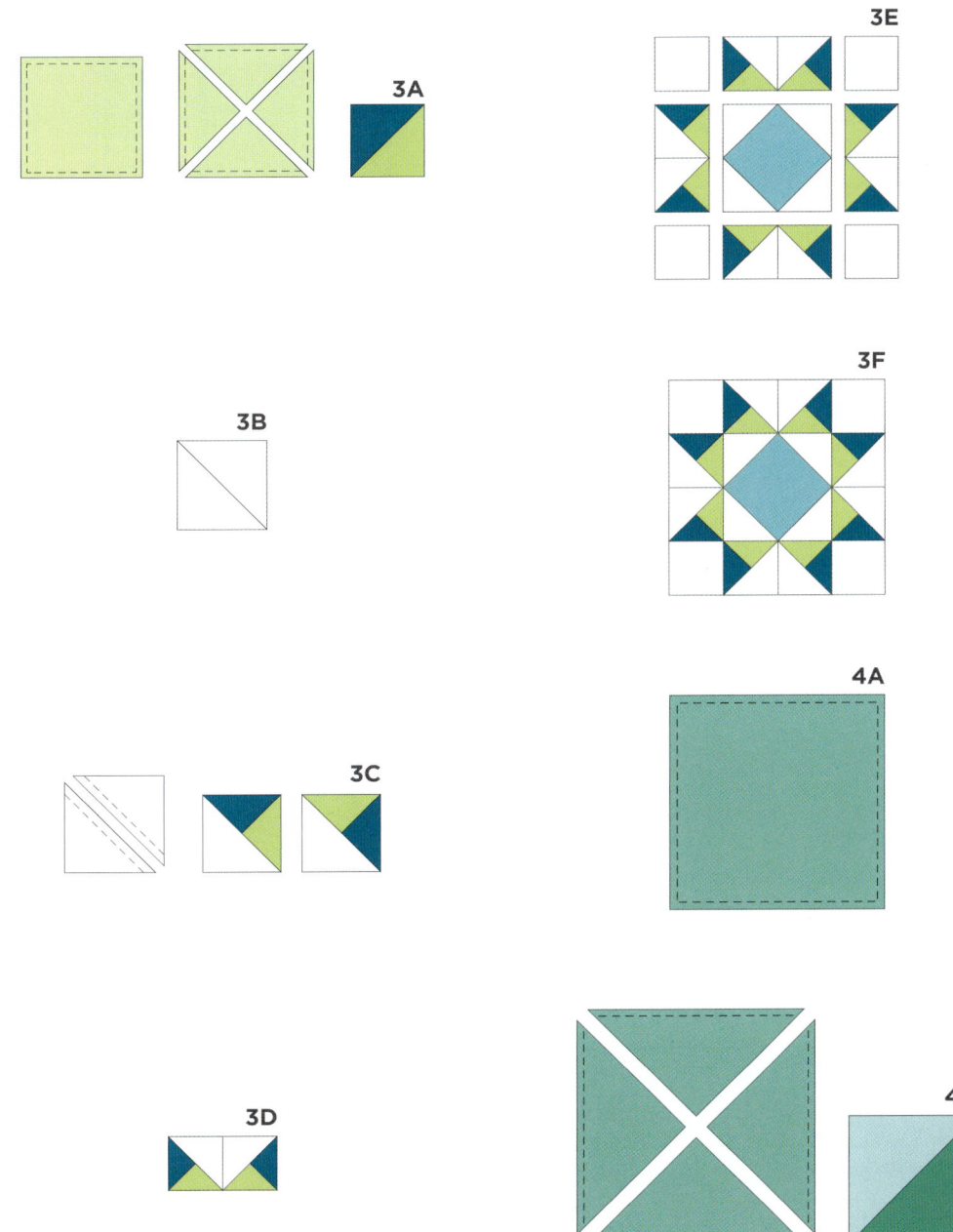

Lay a marked background square atop a half-square triangle with the drawn line crossing over the seam of the half-square triangle. Sew ¼" away from the drawn line on both sides. Cut on the drawn line. If you are using the trimmer, lay your unit with the quarter-square triangle seam facing up. Match the centerline of the trimmer with the seam and trim each unit to 2½", then open and press. If you are not using the slotted trimmer, open each unit and press, then measure 1¼" from the center and trim to 2½" square. **Make 8**. **3C**

Sew 2 units together as shown. Notice the fabric placement is reflected in both units. Press. **Make 4** star leg units. **3D**

Arrange (4) 2½" background squares, 4 star leg units, and a center square as shown. **3E**

Sew the small Missouri Star together in rows. Press the top and bottom rows towards the background squares and the middle row towards the center square. Nest the seams and sew the rows together. Press. **Make 12**. **3F**

4 block construction

Lay 2 unmatching 10" print squares 1 atop of the other, right sides facing. Sew around the perimeter. Cut the sewn squares twice diagonally. Open to reveal 4 large half-square triangles. Press. Do not trim. **4A 4B**

Draw a line from corner to corner once on the diagonal on the reverse side of each 6" background square. **4C**

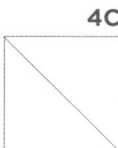

Lay a marked background square atop a large half-square triangle with the drawn line crossing over the seam of the half-square triangle. Sew ¼" away from the drawn line on both sides. Cut on the drawn line. Measure and trim as before, this time to 4½" square. **Make 8**. **4D**

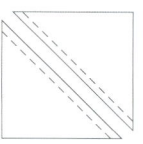  

Sew 2 units together as shown. Notice the fabric placement is reflected in both units. Press. **Make 4** large star leg units. **4E**

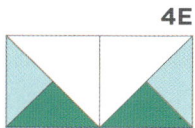

Arrange (4) 4½" background squares, 4 large star leg units, and a small Missouri Star as shown. **4F**

Sew the block together in rows. Press the top and bottom rows towards the background squares and the middle row towards the center. Nest the seams and sew the rows together. Press. **Make 12**. **4G**

Block Size: 16½" unfinished, 16" finished

5 arrange & sew

Refer to the diagram on page 25 to lay out your units in **4 rows of 3 blocks**. Sew the blocks together in rows. Press the seams in opposite directions. Nest the seams and sew the rows together. Press.

6 border

Cut (7) 6" strips across the width of the border fabric. Sew the strips together to make 1 long strip. Trim the borders from this strip. Refer to Borders (pg. 118) in the Construction Basics to measure, cut, and attach the borders. The strip lengths are approximately 64½" for the sides and 59½" for the top and bottom.

7 quilt & bind

Layer the quilt with batting and backing, then quilt. See Construction Basics (pg. 118) to add binding and finish your quilt.

How to Build a Fabric Stash
Supernova Quilt

When I began quilting, I had no idea what fabrics to choose. In fact, my teacher took me out to select the fabrics I needed for my first quilt. Since then, many things have changed. I have developed a style of my own and found fabrics and designers that speak to me. It's thrilling to realize the incredible possibilities that exist in the quilting world! There are so many different styles, patterns, and colors. You can take any pattern and make it your own with your unique fabric choices. So, what fabrics did you first start sewing with? Chances are, you've moved beyond that style to something else. Why did your style change?

Only you know the answer to that question, but my guess is that you became aware of all the possibilities out there and your design sensibilities shifted as a result. When you look at your fabric stash now, does it reflect your current design aesthetic, or does it speak to an older style you no longer love? What should your stash really look like and how can you make it work for you? It can be a challenge to know what is essential, but here are some tips I've gleaned over the years.

I tend to go right for medium value fabric. Most fabric we buy tends to be medium value because it's comfortable. But to make more dynamic quilts, we should be looking for low, medium, and high value. You can discern value just by squinting your eyes. If it's low value, it disappears into the quilt. If it's high value, it stands out. The contrast between your fabrics should be balanced for an interesting quilt design. If it's all medium value, the contrast completely disappears when you squint at your quilt. As you build your fabric stash, be aware of this and don't shy away from those low-volume and high-volume fabrics to make the most of what you have.

Now, we all know our favorite color. We probably have lots of it in our stash. As you build up your stash, look to the right and left of this fabric color on the color wheel to fill in your stash and work with what you love. It's helpful to also think about complementary colors. If you adore lavender, remember that yellows pair beautifully with this color. If you can't get enough blues, try out a daring orange and suddenly that blue will pop! The color wheel can be your best friend.

If you're wondering how much fabric to buy, I would recommend sticking to fat quarters at first. It's incredible how much you can get out of a quarter yard. Consider buying half yards of solids and fabrics you know will be used in multiple projects. Then, buy full yards of fabric you totally love. If you sense that a fabric would make a good quilt backing, that's when you'll want four yards or more. I would also recommend keeping precut packs of solids on hand in neutral colors or even rainbow packs. Those get so much use and they never go out of style. Charm packs are a good way to introduce new colors into your life without spending a lot of cash.

If you like prints, be sure to shop from a variety of fabric lines and really fill out your collection. Don't be afraid to venture outside of your comfort zone and explore new designers and styles. And here's a word to the wise; if you see a print you LOVE, don't skip it! You may not be able to find it easily again.

My final piece of advice for stash building is USE it! You'll love your stash more now than later. If you save a print for too long, it may not be in style anymore and you may not enjoy it as much in a few years. Life's short. Use the pretty fabric!

materials

QUILT SIZE
49½" x 60½"

BLOCK SIZE
6" unfinished, 5½" finished

QUILT TOP
1 package of 10" print squares
2¼ yards of background fabric

BINDING
½ yard

BACKING
3¼ yards - horizontal seam(s)

OTHER
Clearly Perfect Slotted Trimmer B
 - optional

SAMPLE QUILT
Sunprint by Alison Glass for Andover Fabric

1 sort & cut

From the 10" print squares, choose 6 squares for half-square triangles and 12 squares for quarter-square triangles. Set the remaining squares aside for another project.

From the background fabric:
- Cut (2) 10" strips across the width of the fabric. Subcut a **total of (6)** 10" squares.

- Cut (4) 6" strips across the width of the fabric. Subcut a **total of (27)** 6" squares.

- Cut (4) 6¾" strips across the width of the fabric. Subcut a **total of (24)** 6¾" squares.

2A

2B

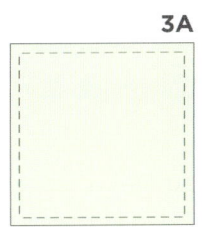
3A

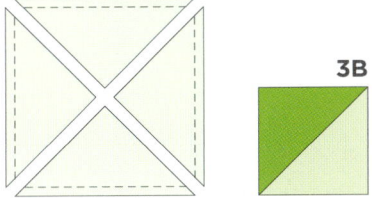
3B

2 make the half-square triangles

Layer a 10" background square atop a 10" print square, right sides facing. Sew around the perimeter. Cut the sewn squares twice diagonally. Use the trimmer to square each unit to 6" then press open—or press, then square to 6" if you're not using the trimmer. **Make 24** half-square triangles. Keep 4 matching blocks together. **2A 2B**

Block Size: 6" unfinished, 5½" finished

3 make the quarter-square triangles

Lay 2 unmatching 10" print squares atop 1 another, right sides facing.

Sew around the perimeter. Cut the sewn squares twice diagonally. Open to reveal 4 half-square triangles. Press. Do not trim. **3A 3B**

Draw a line on the diagonal on the reverse side of each 6¾" background square. **3C**

Layer a marked background square with a half-square triangle, making sure that the drawn line crosses over the seam on the half-square triangle. Sew ¼" away from the drawn line on both sides.

If you are using the slotted trimmer, lay your unit with the quarter-triangle seam facing up. Match the centerline of the trimmer with the seam and trim each unit to 6", then open and press. If you are not using the slotted trimmer, open each unit and press, then measure 3" from the center and trim to 6" square. **Make 48**. Keep 1 set of 8 matching blocks together. **3D**

Block Size: 6" unfinished, 5½" finished

1. Layer a 10" background square atop a 10" print square, right sides facing. Sew around the perimeter. Cut the sewn squares twice diagonally. Square each to 6". Make 24 half-square triangles. Keep 4 matching blocks together.

2. Lay 2 unmatching 10" print squares atop 1 another, right sides facing. Sew around the perimeter. Cut the sewn squares twice diagonally. Open to reveal 4 half-square triangles. Press. Do not trim.

3. Draw a line from corner to corner once on the diagonal on the reverse side of each 6¾" background square.

4. Layer a marked background square with a half-square triangle with the drawn line crossing the seam on the half-square triangle. Sew ¼" away from the line on both sides. Trim each unit to 6" and press. Make 48. Keep 1 set of 8 matching blocks together.

3C  **3D**

4 arrange & sew

Refer to the diagram on the left to lay out your blocks and 6" background squares in **11 rows of 9**. Notice that the 4 matching half-square triangle blocks and 8 matching quarter-square triangle blocks form the Missouri Star in the upper right corner. Sew the blocks together in rows. Press the seams in opposite directions. Nest the seams and sew the rows together. Press.

5 quilt & bind

Layer the quilt with batting and backing, then quilt. See Construction Basics (pg. 118) to add binding and finish your quilt.

How to Use Inherited Quilt Blocks

I love rescuing old quilts and quilt blocks. Whenever I see them in antique malls and thrift shops, I can practically hear them calling my name! Take me home. Make me into something beautiful. I can't bear to pass them up, so I collect unfinished quilt tops and stacks of blocks everywhere I go. Finding them feels like an incredible opportunity to complete what someone else began. I like to think that whoever made these wonderfully imperfect, hand-stitched quilt blocks would love to see them made into a finished project. It's an absolute honor to take another quilter's work and create something new.

Because I always have plenty of extra quilt blocks on hand from my endless thrift shopping and from testing quilt blocks, it can be tough to know what to do with them at times. I often don't have quite enough to make even a lap size quilt, but a wall hanging might do nicely. If I only have one or two in good condition, sometimes I frame them to adorn my sewing room wall. If I have an entire quilt, but it's damaged in places, a nice bed runner or set of stockings for the family might be just the thing. There are so many projects that can be created from leftover quilt blocks and tops. Let's dive in and take them from extra to extraordinary!

Measure Up

The first thing to do is gather all of the quilt blocks together, give them a good looking over, press them well, and measure them. Take note of which blocks are larger or smaller. If all of the blocks are a bit wonky, you can square them up so that they will all measure the same size. Start with your smallest block. If it's quite a bit smaller than the rest of the blocks, consider stitching on some fabric strips that match the background of the block and then squaring it to the same size as the rest of the blocks. Once all of your blocks are squared up, it's time to decide what to create!

Plan Your Project

Once you have all your blocks squared up, go ahead and put them up on your design wall or lay them all out together on the floor or on the table. How many you have will definitely help determine what kind of project you can make. If you have enough for a quilt, arrange your blocks as you'd like and add sashing with cornerstones or even star legs. If you're feeling adventurous, try snowballing the corners for an entirely new look.

For blocks with vintage fabrics, take one of your blocks to the quilt shop with you so you can get a nice match on the background fabric if needed, or pull colors from the design to use in the sashing. If you like to shop from home, it might be time to invest in a color card so you can match solids easily as colors tend to look different on a computer screen vs. in person.

If you tend to make a lot of test blocks like me, try to use solids or coordinating fabrics when you test. Despite the blocks being very different, they will blend well in a sampler quilt. I think these types of quilts look so neat. It's a visual history of the quilt blocks you've attempted over the years. Even if your blocks aren't perfect, in fact, especially if they're not perfect, it's a way to mark your progress.

Smaller Projects

If you find that you don't have enough blocks for an entire quilt, there are many other things you can do with inherited or extra quilt blocks. Here are some fun ideas:

Quilt Labels

Only one block leftover? Put it to great use as a quilt label on the back of the quilt. Appliqué it into a corner after you've recorded all the necessary details like who made the quilt, when, where, and why.

Pieced Quilt Backs

Party in the back! Don't let the front of your quilt have all the fun. Let loose and add a few leftover blocks to your pieced backing for a design that's appealing no matter which side you look at.

Framed Quilt Art

Blocks that are threadbare and won't hold up to washing might not make a good quilt, but you could frame them and hang them up in your home so you can keep on enjoying them for years to come. Sturdier blocks can be pieced together and stapled to canvas stretcher bars for custom wall art that's sure to impress.

Bed & Table Runners

Quilt tops that are damaged can be cut apart and used to make darling bed or table runners. If you have a few larger blocks leftover, they also work well for this purpose.

Wall Hangings

Create a mini quilt for your wall with a few extra blocks to pretty up any room. This is a great idea as well if you have blocks that are a bit delicate. Add fusible, quilt them, and let them shine as art.

Place Mats & Coasters

Set the table for a lovely meal with custom place mats created out of leftover quilt blocks. You can even make a set of cute coasters from smaller blocks.

Throw Pillows

Larger quilt blocks make wonderful throw pillow covers, or you can group together smaller quilt blocks to cover a pillow of any size and bring a touch of comfort to your living room.

Pincushions
Singular quilt blocks make marvelous pin cushions. Stitch them together, add crushed walnut shells inside for stuffing, and you're set. You can also create a cute pincushion with a vintage planter or a ceramic pot. We've even made them with our Thimble Cups!

Christmas Stockings
This is a great project for those larger "cutter" quilts that have enough damage that they can't be salvaged as a whole. Use smaller portions to create a set of matching stockings for the entire family.

Zippered Pouches
We can't get enough zipper pouches and we're guessing you can't either. Take two quilt blocks, add some backing and fusible interfacing, and stitch them together with a Fancy Zip to bring it all together!

Caring for Older Quilts
Once you've finished your beautiful quilt project made up of antique blocks, it will require some special care. Here are some tips to keep in mind when cleaning and storing your quilts.

Washing Your Quilts
Washing a quilt in the tub by hand may seem like the most gentle method, but believe it or not, it isn't always recommended. If the quilt is larger, the weight of the wet quilt can put stress on older fabrics, so be sure to use a gentle detergent like Soak or Orvus and squeeze out the water like you would with a fine sweater if you want to hand wash. Avoid wringing your quilt. Dry your quilt flat. Dry cleaning isn't advised, especially with cotton fabric.

For machine washing, instead of a typical washing cycle, soak your quilt in your washing machine for a few hours up to overnight. Add in a couple of dye trapping sheets like Shout Color Catchers to catch any excess dye. When you're finished soaking your quilt, spin it in the washing machine. It's perfectly safe to do this and it removes excess water easily. Then, wash your quilt on a gentle or hand wash cycle if you have a front loading machine. Rinse your quilt once more to remove any remaining soap. Try not to wash older quilts in machines with agitators. If necessary, take a trip to the local laundromat to use a front loading machine.

To dry your quilt, skip the dryer. Instead, lay your quilt flat on a sheet outdoors or on a bed and turn on a fan over the quilt to speed the drying time. Turn the quilt over after several hours. Instead of folding up your quilt right away, leave it out and unfolded for a few days to make sure it's completely dry. If necessary, air dry the quilt in the dryer for a short time. Try not to wash your quilts too often to prolong their life.

Storing Your Quilts

When you're ready to store your quilt, you can fold it the Missouri Star way or you can store it flat on a spare bed covered with a flat sheet. Keep them out of direct sunlight and store them at a living temperature, not too hot and not too cold. If your attic gets muggy or your basement is chilly, don't store quilts there. Keep quilts in an environment where they can breathe, so it's best to avoid plastic storage totes and plastic bags. You can store quilts in cedar chests, but make sure the wood is finished. Wood and paper can be acidic and will break down fabric over time.

If you enjoy hanging your quilts for display, go for it! Hang your quilt so that its evenly supported across the top edge with a rod or dowel. And here's a handy tip: When you add a hanging sleeve, add one to both the top and bottom of your quilt and rotate it a couple times a year. If you like to fold your quilts and display them on chairs, shelves, or beds, rotate the quilts you have on display several times a year.

Best in Show
Playground Quilt

Cookies, like quilts, are so much better when they're made with love.

October 1st is National Homemade Cookies Day, so Camille, a member of our team, shared memories of learning to bake at her Grandmother's side. Maybe her story is a bit like yours:

"When I was a kid, summer time was sprinkled with visits to Grandma's house to work on 4-H projects that could be sent to the county fair.

"First up was a pair of bright pink shorts. Grandma showed me how to pin a paper pattern to fabric and cut as neatly as my little hands could manage. I remember tackling the curvy crotch seam and threading elastic through the waistband. Grandma insisted I pause to press between each and every step.

"Next, we started canning. Grandma always saved me the prettiest fruits and vegetables from her garden. We filled pint jars with extra long green beans. They stood tall and straight like little soldiers, packed snug and neat together.

"We stood over bubbling pots of fresh raspberry jam that, despite my best efforts, sputtered lava-hot droplets on my hands and arms. Gingerly, we poured the steaming jam into quilted half pints, careful to strain out some of the seeds. 'Judges don't like a lot of seeds,' Grandma always said.

"We blanched peaches in a sinkful of scalding-hot water, then pulled off the fuzzy orange skin. The peaches were sliced in half and nested in big quart jars—always with the pretty, smooth sides facing out. We wiped the bottles clean before topping them with lids and shining, gold rings.

"Last of all, at the very end of summer, came the baking. The day before the fair was a flurry of flour and sugar, and everything had to be just so. I filled measuring cups to overflowing before leveling them off with a knife. I carefully sifted and stirred. Grandma inspected each ball of cookie dough for precise roundness before they were tossed into a bowl of cinnamon sugar and baked for exactly ten minutes. I remember hovering over cooling racks, searching for four snickerdoodles that were perfectly golden and exactly the same size. Only the best for the fair!

"At the time, the ultimate prize for all this work was a handful of blue ribbons and the occasional 'Best In Show' rosette. Many of my projects even made it all the way to the state fair. But now, years and years later, I can see that the sweetest reward was time spent with Grandma. We weren't just making cookies; we were making memories."

Best in Show Snickerdoodles

1 cup butter, softened	2 tsp. cream of tartar
1½ cups white sugar	1 tsp. baking soda
2 eggs	½ tsp. salt
2 tsp. vanilla extract	2 tbsp. white sugar
2¾ cups all-purpose flour	2 tbsp. ground cinnamon

Preheat oven to 400° F. Cream together butter, sugar, eggs, and vanilla. Sift together flour, cream of tartar, baking soda, and salt. Combine the dry ingredients with the wet ingredients. Roll dough into 1" balls. Mix 2 tbsp. sugar and 2 tbsp. cinnamon together. Thoroughly coat balls of dough with cinnamon sugar. Place cookies 2" apart on an ungreased baking sheet. Bake 10 minutes or until set, but not browned. Enjoy!

materials

QUILT SIZE
59" x 59"

BLOCK SIZE
12½" unfinished, 12" finished

QUILT TOP
1 package 10" print squares
1 roll of 2½" background strips

BORDER
1¼ yards

BINDING
¾ yard

BACKING
3¾ yards - horizontal seam(s)

SAMPLE QUILT
Artisan Batiks Evening Glow
 by Lunn Studios for Robert Kaufman

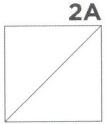

2A

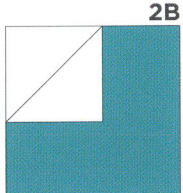

2B

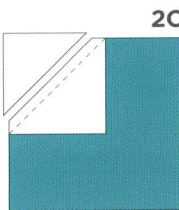

2C

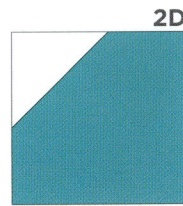

2D

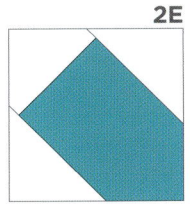

2E

1 sort & cut

Sort your package of 10" print squares into 3 stacks. Be sure to choose a variety of colors for each stack.

- Stack A is made up of 16 squares and will be used for the block corners.

- Stack B is made up of 16 squares and will be used for the outer flying geese and block centers.

- Stack C is made up of 10 squares and will be used for the inner flying geese.

From each of the 10" squares in Stack A, cut (2) 4½" strips across the width of each square. Subcut a **total of (64)** 4½" squares from the strips. Keep the matching squares together.

From each of the 10" squares in Stack B:
- Cut (2) 2½" strips across the width of each square. Subcut (4) 2½" squares from the strips for a **total of 128**.

- From the remainder of each square, cut (1) 5" x 4½" rectangle. Trim each of the 16 rectangles to 4½" square.

- Set the remainder of each square aside for another project.

From each of the 10" squares in Stack C, cut (2) 4½" strips. Subcut a **total of (80)** 4½" x 2½" rectangles from the strips. Keep these organized in 16 sets of 4 matching rectangles. **Note**: You will have 16 extra flying geese units that can be set aside for another project.

From the roll of 2½" background strips:
- Cut 8 strips into (8) 2½" x 4½" rectangles each for a **total of 64**.

- Cut 24 strips into (16) 2½" squares each for a **total of 384**.

- Set the remaining strips aside for another project.

2 snowball corners

Mark a diagonal line on the reverse side of each 2½" background square.
Note: 128 marked squares will be used in section 3. **2A**

Place a marked background square on a corner of a 4½" Stack A square, right sides facing, as shown. **2B**

Sew on the marked line. Trim the excess fabric ¼" away from the seam. Press. **2C 2D**

Repeat to snowball 3 corners of the square. **2E**

1. Mark a diagonal line on each 2½" background square. Place a marked square on 1 corner of a 4½" print square. Sew on the marked line, then trim and press.

2. Place 2 marked squares on the adjacent corners. Sew on the marked lines, then trim and press. Make 4.

3. Place 2 marked squares on opposite corners of a 4½" print square. Sew on the marked lines, then trim and press. Place 2 marked squares on the remaining corners of the 4½" square and repeat.

4. Place a marked square on 1 end of a 4½" x 2½" print rectangle as shown. Sew on the marked line, then trim and press. Repeat on the other end of the rectangle. Make 4 inner flying geese units.

5. Mark a diagonal line on the reverse side of (8) 2½" print squares. Repeat the previous steps to make 4 outer flying geese units. Sew an outer flying geese unit to the top of an inner flying geese unit and press. Make 4.

6. Arrange the units you have made in 3 rows of 3 as shown. Sew the units together in rows. Press the seams in opposite directions. Nest the seams and sew the rows together. Make 16 blocks.

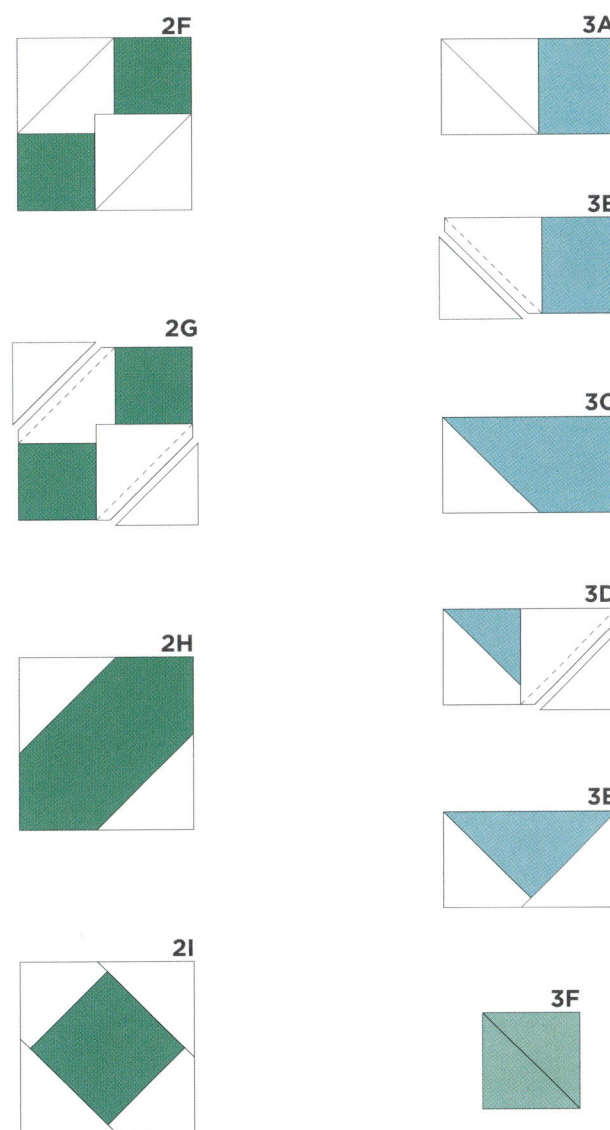

Repeat with all remaining Stack A squares to **make 64** corner units. Keep the matching units together in sets of 4.

Place a marked background square on 2 opposite corners of a 4½" Stack B square, right sides facing, as shown. **2F**

Sew on the marked lines. Trim the excess fabric ¼" away from the seams. Press. **2G 2H**

Repeat to snowball the 2 remaining corners of the square. **2I**

Make 16 center squares.

3 make the flying geese

Place a 2½" marked background square on the end of a 4½" x 2½" Stack C rectangle, right sides facing, as shown. **3A**

Sew on the marked line. Trim the excess fabric ¼" away from the seam. Press. **3B 3C**

Place another 2½" marked background square on the opposite end of the unit, right sides facing, as shown. Sew on the marked line, trim, and press as before. **3D 3E**

Make 64 inner flying geese units and keep the matching units together in sets of 4.

Mark a diagonal line on the reverse side of each 2½" Stack B square. **3F**

Repeat the instructions above using the marked Stack B squares and 2½" x 4½" background rectangles to **make 64** outer flying geese units. Keep matching units together in sets of 4. **3G**

4 block construction

Pick up 1 set of 4 corner units, 1 set of 4 outer flying geese units, 1 set of 4 inner flying geese units, and 1 center square that matches the outer flying geese units.

Sew an outer flying geese unit to the top of an inner flying geese unit as shown. **Make 4** units. **4A**

Arrange the units in 3 rows of 3 as shown. **4B**

Sew the units together to form rows. Press the seams in opposite directions. Nest the seams and sew the rows together. **Make 16**. **4C**

Block Size: 12½" unfinished, 12" finished

5 arrange & sew

Refer to the diagram on the next page to layout the blocks in **4 rows of 4**. Sew the blocks together to form the rows. Press in the rows in opposite directions. Nest the seams and sew the rows together. Press.

6 border

From the border fabric, cut (6) 6" strips across the width of the fabric. Sew the strips together to form 1 long strip. Cut the borders from this strip. Refer to Borders (pg. 118) in the Construction Basics to measure, cut, and attach the borders. The strip lengths should be approximately 48½" for the sides and 59½" for the top and bottom.

7 quilt & bind

Layer the quilt with batting and backing, then quilt. See Construction Basics (pg. 118) to add binding and finish your quilt.

Generations of Quilters

Pinwheel Frolic Quilt
by Duon Zeroun, a Customer Story

I grew up with quilts and have always admired their colors and patterns, but there are two family quilts that have touched my heart, and I'd like to share their stories with you now:

The Courting Quilt: When I was thirteen years old, my mother took us to visit her hometown of Mound City, Missouri. Her relatives settled the town during the 1820s, and in 1900, my great-grandfather became a representative in the state legislature.

While visiting this tiny town, we met my grandfather's sister. We sat on the front porch drinking ice-cold tea, and she told me about a quilt that her great grandparents had stitched together while courting on that very same porch. I could hardly imagine a young couple quilting on a date!

My great-aunt disappeared inside the house and reemerged with the quilt in her arms. It was a cream-colored wholecloth quilt covered with tiny delicate stitches—stitches that had been placed by my very own great-great-grandparents. I fell in love.

When my great-aunt passed, her quilts were divided among relatives, but there was no sign of the courting quilt. I always think of that quilt and hope it went to a good home.

The Tree of Life Quilt: When I was a young mother, I opened an old chest at my parents' house and discovered a quilt top made of shirts, dresses, flour sacks, and tea sacks in a very scrappy Tree of Life pattern. It had been made by my father's side of the family, who had survived the Great Depression by learning to "make do."

I secretly took the quilt top home, found a sheet backing, and basted it all together. Every, night after putting the children to bed, I quilted. And as I quilted, I pored over the fabric, imagining whose shirts and dresses they came from. I gave the finished quilt to my parents for Christmas, who loved and used it for the next twenty-five years. Now it is mine, but that is not the end of the story.

In 2019, my father's sister celebrated her 100th birthday. My cousin found three quilts in the back bedroom, and there among the quilts was a quilt top that was identical to the top I had finished for my parents forty-five years before.

I did some detective work and discovered that the quilt tops were made for my dad and his sister by my grandmother, my great-grandmother, and my great-aunts. My cousin has kept hers in Texas and I keep mine in California, but I would love to reunite these two quilts some day.

Quilts have certainly touched generations of my family, and now I am teaching my own grandchildren to sew and quilt. I have written the stories of these quilts and the women who made them.

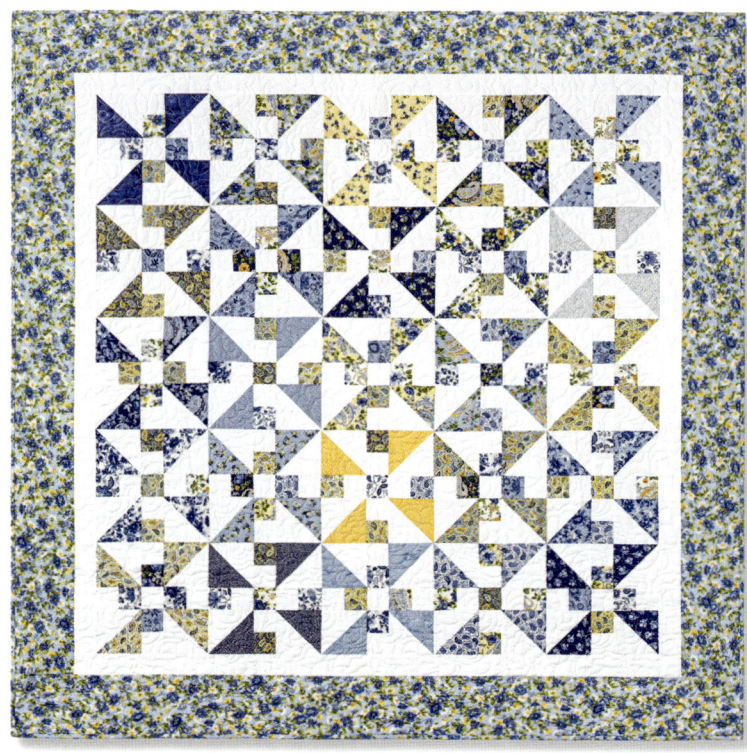

materials

QUILT SIZE
65" x 65"

BLOCK SIZE
10½" unfinished, 10" finished

QUILT TOP
2 packages of 5" print squares
2 packages of
   5" background squares

INNER BORDER
½ yard

OUTER BORDER
1¼ yards

BINDING
¾ yard

BACKING
4¼ yards - vertical seam(s)
   or 2¼ yards of 108" wide

SAMPLE QUILT
Summer Breeze
   by Moda Fabrics

1 make the half-square triangles

Mark a diagonal line on the reverse side of (50) 5" background squares. **1A**

Lay a marked square atop a 5" print square, right sides facing. Sew ¼" away from the marked line on both sides. Cut on the marked line. Open, press, then trim each unit to 4½". **1B 1C**

Use a matching 5" print square and another marked background square to create a **total of 4** matching half-square triangles. Keep the 4 matching half-square triangles together in a set.

Repeat to **make 25** sets of 4 matching half-square triangles.

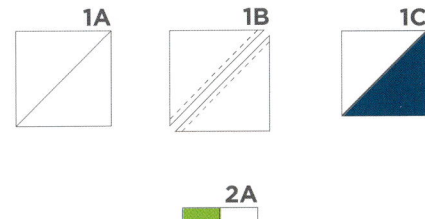

2 make the 2-patches

Select (28) 5" print squares and (29) 5" background squares. Cut each square in half vertically and horizontally for a **total of (112)** 2½" print squares and (116) 2½" background squares. Set (3) 2½" background squares aside for another project leaving you with a **total of (113)** 2½" background squares.

Sew a 2½" print square to a 2½" background square. Press towards the darker fabric. **Make 100**. **2A**

3 block A construction

Pick up a set of 4 matching half-square triangles, (4) 2-patch units each with different prints, and a 2½" background square. Arrange the units in 3 rows of 3 as shown. **3A**

Sew the units together to form rows. Press. Nest the seams and sew the rows together to form block A. **Make 13**. **3B**

Block Size: 10½" unfinished, 10" finished

4 block B construction

Pick up a set of 4 matching half-square triangles, (4) 2-patch units each with different prints, and a 2½" print square. Arrange the units in 3 rows of 3 as shown. **4A**

Sew the units together to form rows. Press. Nest the seams and sew the rows together to form block B. **Make 12**. **4B**

Block Size: 10½" unfinished, 10" finished

5 arrange & sew

Refer to the diagram on page 51 to layout the blocks in **5 rows of 5**.

Hint: The first row starts with an A block and the A and B blocks alternate from there.

Sew the blocks together to form the rows.

1. Mark a diagonal line on the reverse side of the 5″ background squares. Lay a marked square atop a 5″ print square, right sides facing. Sew on both sides of the marked line. Cut on the line, open, and press.

2. Sew a 2½″ print square to a 2½″ background square to make a 2-patch unit.

3. Lay 4 matching half-square triangles, (4) 2-patch units with different prints, and a 2½″ background square in 3 rows of 3 as shown.

4. Sew the units together in rows. Press in opposite directions. Nest the seams and sew the rows together to create a block A. Make 13.

5. Lay 4 matching half-square triangles, (4) 2-patch units with different prints, and a 2½″ print square in 3 rows of 3 as shown.

6. Sew the units together in rows. Press in opposite directions. Nest the seams and sew the rows together to create a block B. Make 12.

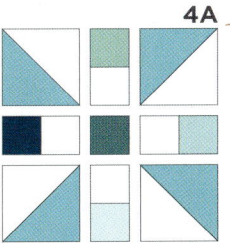

Press the rows in opposite directions. Nest the seams and sew the rows together. Press.

6 inner border

From the inner border fabric, cut (6) 2½" strips across the width of the fabric. Sew the strips together to form 1 long strip. Cut the inner borders from this strip. Refer to Borders (pg. 118) in the Construction Basics to measure, cut, and attach the inner borders. The strip lengths should be approximately 50½" for the sides and 54½" for the top and bottom.

7 outer border

From the outer border fabric, cut (6) 6" strips across the width of the fabric. Sew the strips together to form 1 long strip. Cut the outer borders from this strip. Refer to Borders (pg. 118) in the Construction Basics to measure, cut, and attach the outer borders. The strip lengths should be approximately 54½" for the sides and 65½" for the top and bottom.

8 quilt & bind

Layer the quilt with batting and backing, then quilt. See Construction Basics (pg. 118) to finish your quilt.

More Than Pretty Fabric
Goose Tracks Quilt

Helping those with breast cancer is a cause near and dear to our hearts. Chances are you know someone or are someone who has been affected by this disease. One in eight women will develop breast cancer in their lifetime. Because October is Breast Cancer Awareness Month, we want to spotlight a quilter named Joanne Cross. Here's her story:

"I love to quilt. I made each one of my nine coworkers a quilt for their birthdays during 2019. In March of 2021, one young pharmacist, Marilyn, at 34 years of age, told us she was diagnosed with breast cancer. The news was devastating. Her career as a pharmacist had just started. She has a beautiful young family with two daughters, aged 3 years and 5 years old, and a wonderful, supportive husband.

"Marilyn and her group of doctors came up with a treatment plan. From April to August 2021, she was treated with radiation and chemotherapy. She will have reconstructive breast surgery in October 2021. And yet, she is still coming to work everyday! Marilyn has a port to receive her medication and no hair, but the cutest wig ever! Her smile can brighten any room she's in. The twinkle in her eyes is breathless! She is one super amazing person. I tell you from my heart that God truly smiled the day she was born.

"I had seen Jenny's Breast Cancer Ribbon quilt tutorial a few years ago. At the time, Missouri Star Quilt Co. was offering a kit to make the quilt.

I purchased one kit. It sat in my quilting room for over two years. I had often thought about making it. Deep inside I just didn't want to. It meant that the person I would give it to would have breast cancer. But the pink colors, shaped in a ribbon, were just so pretty!

"When Marilyn told us her diagnosis, I knew instantly my quilt would have a purpose! It had waited for the right time and the right person to receive it.

"As I constructed and sewed this beautiful quilt, my thoughts of so many happy times during our work days flooded my mind. I smiled, laughed, and cried during the sewing of her pink ribbon quilt. The quilt took me two days—Saturday and Sunday—to finish. When I finished, my local quilter sped up the turnaround time to finish it. My quilter gave it back to me in less than a week! See, we in the quilting community bond together for special quilts. Aren't we quilters all so awesome together?

"I prayed and laid hands on this wonderful quilt to give Marilyn comfort, warmth, love, healing, and endless hugs. Marilyn was overwhelmed when I gave the quilt to her. Of course, we hugged and teared up. She told me she's taking it to her treatments to snuggle under. How wonderful.

"You see, a quilt is more than pretty fabric. It has a life of its own. A purpose. A memory. A timeline in our lives."

materials

QUILT SIZE
73" x 73"

BLOCK SIZE
18½" unfinished, 18" finished

QUILT TOP
3 packages of 5" print squares
1½ yards of background fabric
 - includes inner border

OUTER BORDER
1¾ yards

BINDING
1 yard

BACKING
4½ yards - vertical seam(s)
 or 2¼ yards of 108" wide

OTHER
Scallops, Vines & Waves
 Template for Quilt in a Day®
The Bias Binding Tool
 for TQM Products

SAMPLE QUILT
Bluebird by Edyta Sitar
 of Laundry Basket Quilts
 for Andover Fabric

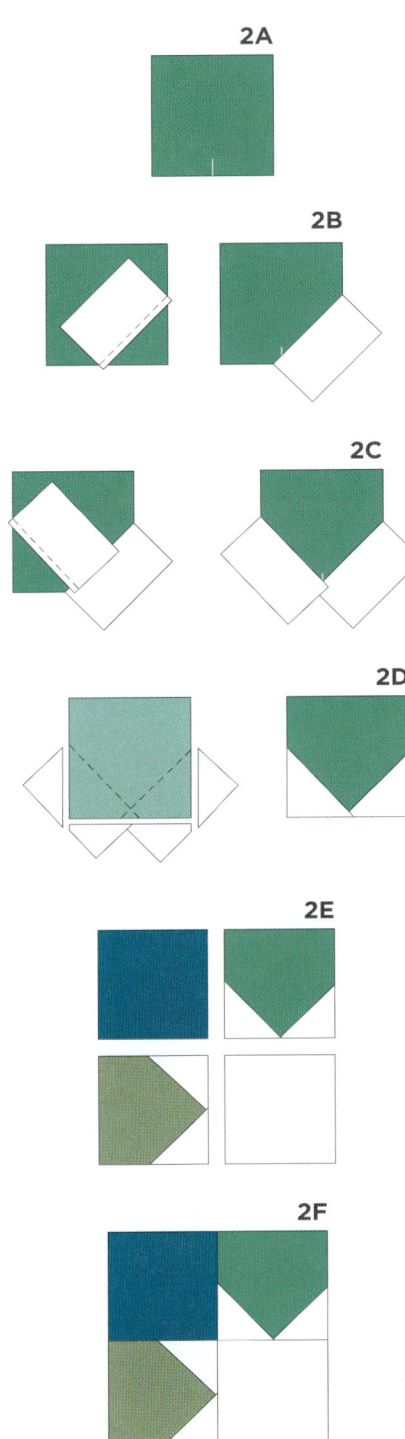

1 cut

From the background fabric:

- Cut (3) 5″ strips across the width of the fabric. Subcut (8) 5″ squares from each of 2 strips. Subcut (2) 5″ squares from the remaining strip for a **total of (18)** 5″ squares. Trim the remainder of the strip to 4″ for the next cutting step.

- Cut (4) 4″ strips across the width of the fabric. From the full and partial 4″ strips, subcut a **total of (72)** 4″ x 2½″ rectangles. Set the remaining fabric aside for the inner border.

2 make the goose tracks

Fold 1 edge of a 5″ print square in half and crease to mark the center. **2A**

Lay a 4″ x 2½″ background rectangle atop the marked square as shown. The 2 corners of the rectangle should slightly overlap the marked center and go about halfway up the side of the square. Sew along the edge of the rectangle as shown. Press over the corner. **2B**

Repeat to add another rectangle to the opposite side as shown. **2C**

Turn the sewn unit over and trim the edges even with the square. **Make 36** goose toes units. **2D**

Arrange 2 goose toes units, (1) 5″ print square, and (1) 5″ background square in 2 rows of 2 as shown. No print should be repeated. Sew the units together in rows and press towards the squares. Nest the seams and sew the rows together. Press. **Make 18** goose track units. **2E 2F**

3 make 4-patches

Arrange 4 different 5″ print squares in 2 rows of 2 as shown. Sew the units together in rows and press in opposite directions. Nest the seams and sew the rows together. Press. **Make 18**. **3A 3B**

4 block construction

Arrange 2 goose track units and (2) 4-patches in 2 rows of 2 as shown. Sew the units together in rows and press towards the 4-patches. Nest the seams and sew the rows together. Press. **Make 9**. **4A 4B**

Block Size: 18½″ unfinished, 18″ finished

5 arrange & sew

Refer to diagram **8A** as necessary to lay out your units in **3 rows of 3 blocks**. Notice the direction of the goose tracks alternate. Sew the blocks together in rows. Press the seams in opposite directions. Nest the seams and sew the rows together. Press.

6 inner border

Cut (6) 2½″ strips across the width of the background fabric. Sew the strips together to make 1 long strip. Trim the borders from this strip. Refer to Borders (pg. 118) in the Construction Basics to measure, cut, and attach the borders. The strip lengths are approximately 54½″ for the sides and 58½″ for the top and bottom.

1. Lay a 4" x 2½" background rectangle atop the marked square as shown. Sew along the edge of the rectangle as shown. Press over the corner.

2. Repeat to add another rectangle to the opposite side as shown. Turn the sewn unit over and trim the edges even with the square to create a goose toes unit.

3. Arrange 2 goose toes units, (1) 5" print square, and (1) 5" background square in 2 rows of 2 as shown. Sew the units together in rows and press towards the squares. Nest the seams and sew the rows together. Press.

4. Arrange 4 different 5" print squares in 2 rows of 2 as shown. Sew the units together in rows and press in opposite directions. Nest the seams and sew the rows together. Press.

5. Arrange 2 goose track units and (2) 4-patches in 2 rows of 2 as shown. Sew the units together in rows and press towards the 4-patches. Nest the seams and sew the rows together. Press.

7 outer border

Cut (7) 8" strips across the width of the outer border fabric. Sew the strips together to make 1 long strip. Trim the borders from this strip. Refer to Borders (pg. 118) in the Construction Basics to measure, cut, and attach the borders. The lengths are approximately 58½" for the sides and 73½" for the top and bottom.

8 quilt & trim

Layer the quilt with batting and backing, then quilt. After the quilting has been completed, use the template to mark the scallops just inside the outer edge of the quilt. (Follow the instructions included in the booklet that comes with the template.) Refer to diagram **8A** as needed and cut the scalloped edges.

9 make the bias binding

Because the edges of this quilt are scalloped, you will need to make bias binding. Cut the binding fabric in half to yield 2 half-yard pieces. Use the bias binding ruler and follow the manufacturer's directions to cut 2½" bias strips that total at least 318" once the strips have been sewn together. Sew the strips together in 1 long strip. Gently press the strip in half, wrong sides together. Sew the binding to the front of the quilt, matching the raw edges of the binding and quilt, and pivoting in the scallop points. Turn the folded binding edge to the back and whipstitch in place to complete your quilt.

Falling for the Season
Breezy Windmills Quilt

Step out onto your porch and take a deep breath. Do you smell that? Crisp leaves and moisture from the light morning dew clinging to every outdoor surface on the fall breeze. Now is the perfect time to sit on the porch swing and take delightful sips of my breakfast tea. The season of change and harvest is upon us, and I can't help but smile about it.

Is autumn your favorite season? It has plenty of reasons to be loved, what with the wonderful variety of scents that accompany the time of year and the comfortable snuggle weather, just cool enough for a light jacket but not so cold that you can't enjoy the fresh air. With spooky time approaching, now is the time to grab a cozy quilt, watch the sun set between orange covered branches, and think about the celebrations to come.

Cuddle up with your friend, a loved one, your children, or your grandchildren and admire the brightly colored trees. Or better yet, rake up a crunchy pile of leaves for the little ones to frolic in, or teach them how to carve a pumpkin. Watch them stick their hands in to scoop out the gooey seeds as the pumpkin's fresh aroma invades your nose.

Decorate the porch in cobwebs and spiders, hangings ghosts and skeletons everywhere. Enjoy some hot apple cider or hot cocoa with mini marshmallows before a hay ride down to the small town pumpkin patch. Go skip rocks at a pond or lake, let the ripples warp the branch reflections in crystalline wavelets and watch until the water settles. Bask in the warmth of a bonfire with friends and family on a chilly night, sharing fond stories and immersing yourselves in the toasty nostalgia.

Now take all of these warm, fuzzy feelings and the colors from your memories and put them onto something more tangible. Recreate those nostalgic moments, the years that have passed you by, the loving remembrance of someone long gone, with a beautifully customized quilt that will always be beside you. Let it keep you warm and safe. Let it take you back to all the falls before this one, to a time when all you needed was to enjoy the cool morning breeze with a hot mug. Let every autumn morning feel peaceful and happy, just like this.

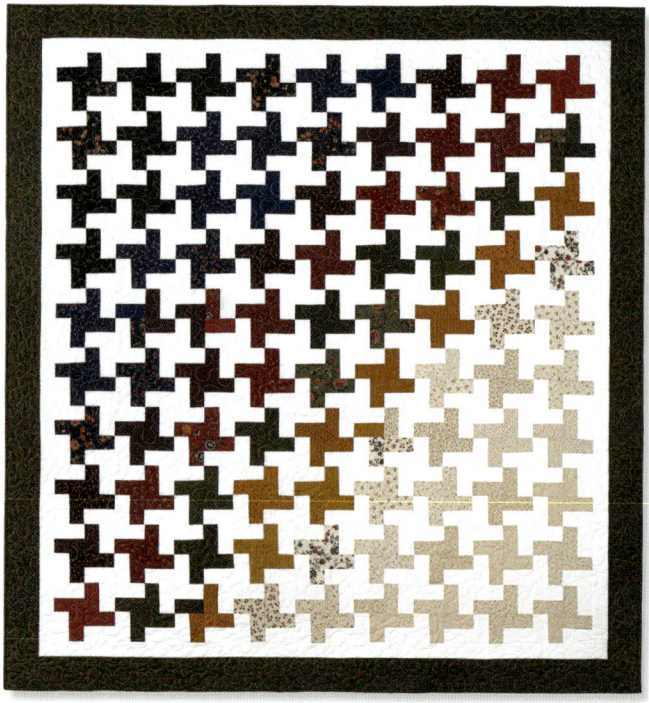

materials

QUILT SIZE
85" x 93"

BLOCK SIZE
8½" unfinished, 8" finished

QUILT TOP
1 roll of 2½" print strips
1 roll of 2½" background strips

INNER BORDER
¾ yard

OUTER BORDER
1½ yards

BINDING
¾ yard

BACKING
8½ yards - vertical seam(s)
or 3 yards of 108" wide

SAMPLE QUILT
Prairie Dreams
by Kansas Troubles Quilters
for Moda Fabrics

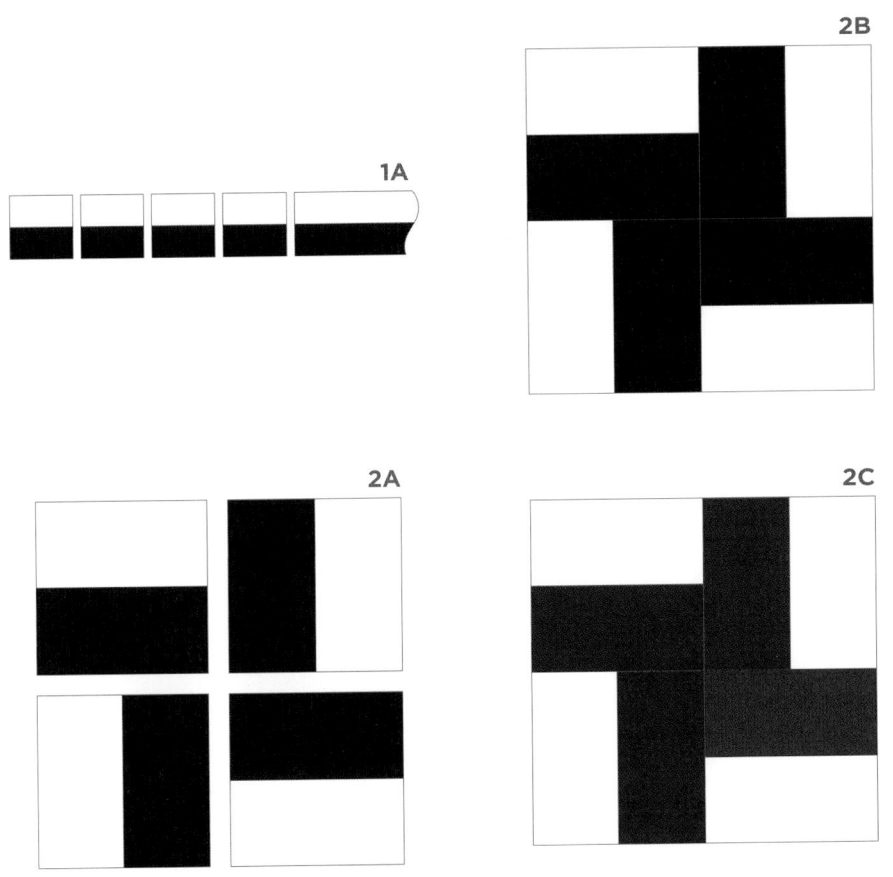

1 make strip units

Sew 1 print strip to 1 background strip, lengthwise. Open and press. **Make 40**.

Cut each strip set into (9) 4½" strip units for a **total of 360**. **1A**

2 block construction

Select 4 units with matching or similar color values. Arrange these in 2 rows of 2. Notice that the print sections of the units meet in the center. **2A**

Sew the units together in rows and press in opposite directions. Nest the seams and sew the rows together. Press. **2B**

As you continue to make blocks with matching or similar color values, you will have some units that do not have 4 matching or similar colors. Arrange 4 of these units so they will transition 1 color to the next in your gradient arrangement. Sew these together in the same manner as before. **2C**

Make 90 blocks.

Block Size: 8½" unfinished, 8" finished

1. Sew 1 print strip to 1 background strip, lengthwise. Open and press. Make 40. Cut each strip set into (9) 4½″ strip units for a total of 360.

2. Select 4 units with matching or similar color values. Arrange these in 2 rows of 2. Notice that the print sections of the units meet in the center.

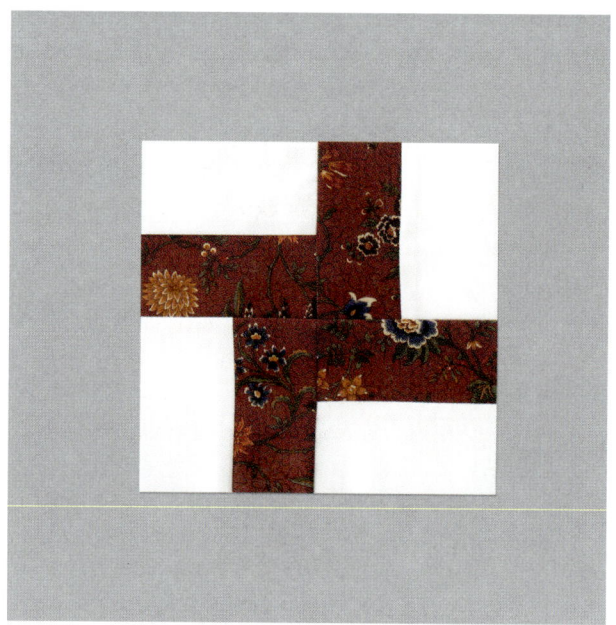

3. Sew the units together in rows and press in opposite directions. Nest the seams and sew the rows together. Press.

4. You will have some units that do not have 4 matching or similar colors. Arrange 4 of these units so they will transition 1 color to the next in your gradient arrangement. Sew these together in the same manner as before.

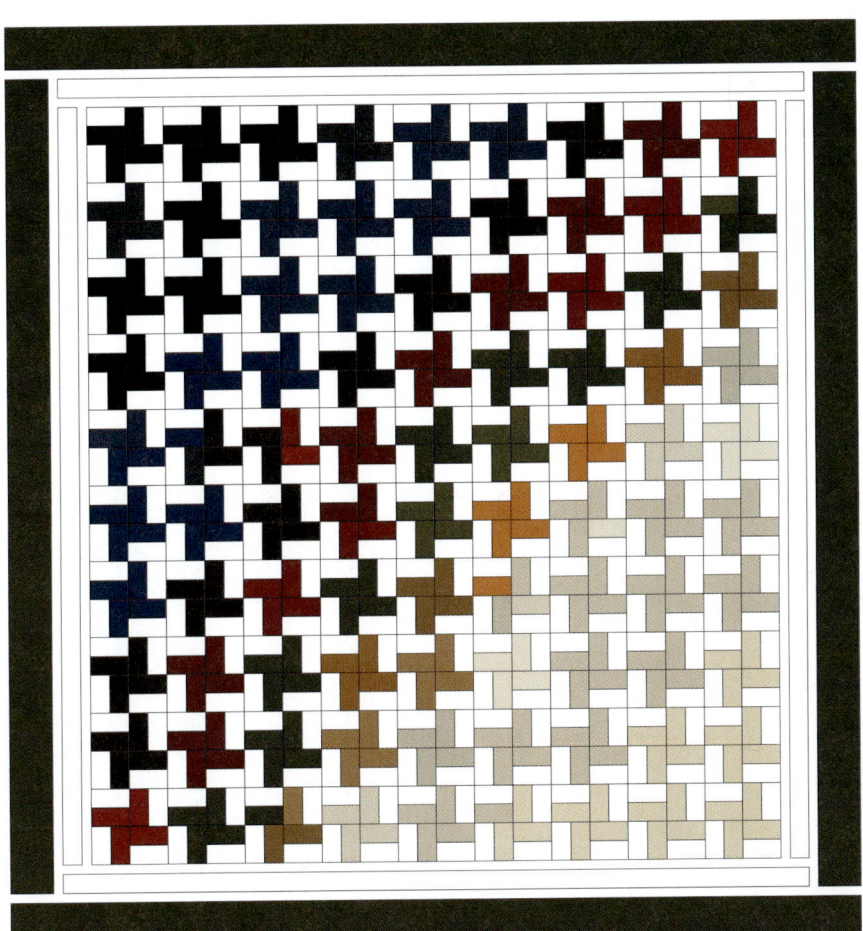

3 arrange & sew

Refer to the diagram on the left as necessary to lay out your units in **10 rows of 9 blocks**. Notice that the gradient layout transitions 1 color to the next. Sew the blocks together in rows. Press the seams in opposite directions. Nest the seams and sew the rows together. Press.

4 inner border

Cut (8) 2½" strips across the width of the inner border fabric. Sew the strips together to make 1 long strip. Trim the borders from this strip. Refer to Borders (pg. 118) in the Construction Basics to measure, cut, and attach the borders. The lengths are approximately 80½" for the sides and 76½" for the top and bottom.

5 outer border

Cut (9) 5" strips across the width of the outer border fabric. Sew the strips together to make 1 long strip. Trim the borders from this strip. Refer to Borders (pg. 118) in the Construction Basics to measure, cut, and attach the borders. The lengths are approximately 84½" for the sides and 85½" for the top and bottom.

6 quilt & bind

Layer the quilt with batting and backing, then quilt. See Construction Basics (pg. 118) to add binding and finish your quilt.

Talavera Tile Sew-Along
PART 5

SUPER EASY HOURGLASS BLOCK SIZE
6¼" unfinished, 5¾" finished

PINWHEEL PARTY BLOCK SIZE
5½" unfinished, 5" finished

BLOCK SUPPLIES - SUPER EASY HOURGLASS
(2) 10" fabric D squares
(2) 10" fabric E squares

BLOCK SUPPLIES - FANCY FLIGHT
(2) 10" fabric C squares
(1) 5" fabric F strip - cut from yardage

Note: Fabrics A, B, and G are not used in Part 5.

SUPER EASY HOURGLASS

PINWHEEL PARTY

QUILT SIZE
77" x 77"

WHOLE QUILT TOP
1 package 10" print squares
1 package of 10" Talavera Tile squares:
- 10 fabric A squares
- 10 fabric B squares
- 7 fabric C squares
- 14 fabric D squares
- 11 fabric E squares

¼ yard fabric B
  - includes Lemon Star border
¼ yard fabric C
1½ yards fabric F
  - includes sashing and Lemon Star border

3¼ yards fabric G
  - includes sashing, Lemon Star border, and binding

BINDING
¾ yard

BACKING
4¾ yards – vertical seam(s) or 2½ yards 108" wide *

Note: 2 packages of 10" print squares can be substituted for the package of Talavera Tile squares. You will need a **total of (52)** 10" squares. Other packages of squares may not have the same number of duplicate prints needed to match the quilt exactly.

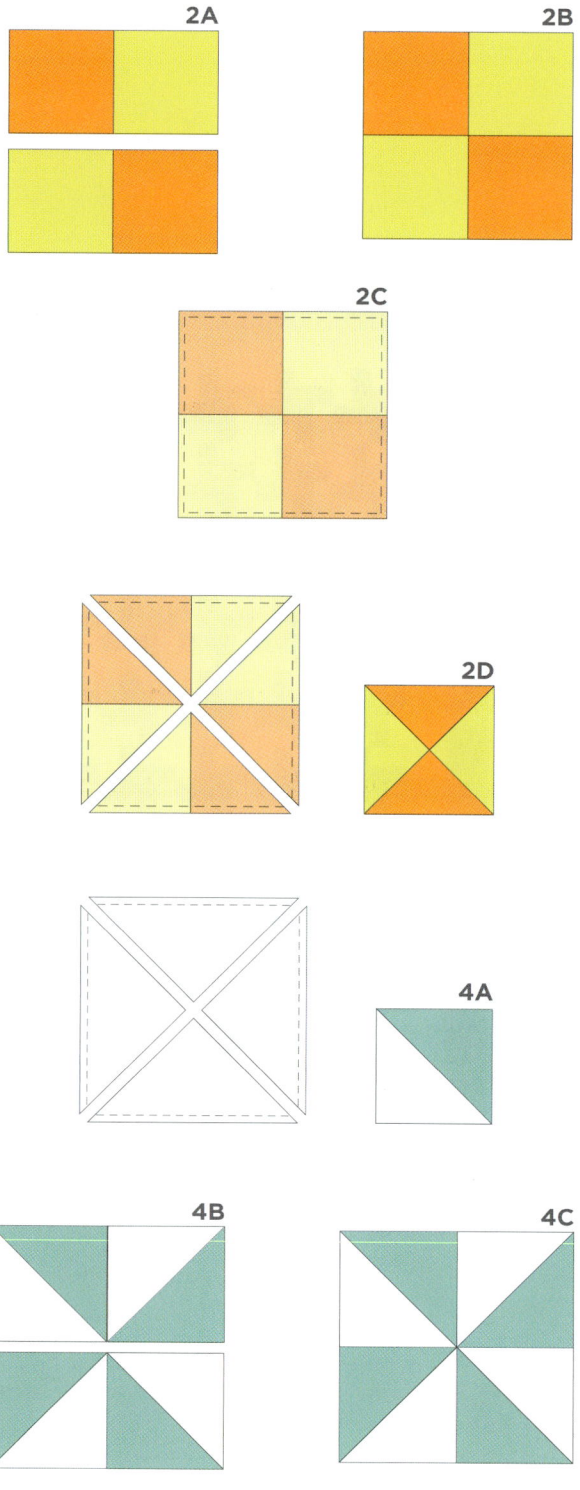

SUPER EASY HOURGLASS

1 cut

Cut each of the fabric D and fabric E squares in half vertically and horizontally to create (4) 5" squares from each for a **total of (8)** 5" fabric D squares and a **total of (8)** 5" fabric E squares.

2 sew

Select 2 fabric D squares and 2 fabric E squares and arrange them in a 4-patch formation as shown. Sew the squares together in 2 rows. Press the seam of each row toward the fabric E square. **2A**

Nest the seams and sew the rows together. Press the center seam to 1 side. **Make 4**. **2B**

Layer (2) 4-patch units together with right sides facing. Make sure each fabric D square faces a fabric E square. Sew all around the outside edge using a scant ¼" seam allowance. **2C**

Cut the sewn unit from corner to corner twice on the diagonal. Open to reveal 4 hourglass blocks. Press. Square each block to 6¼". **2D**

Repeat using the remaining 4-patch units to **make 8** Super Easy Hourglass blocks.

Super Easy Hourglass Block Size: 6¼" unfinished, 5¾" finished

PINWHEEL PARTY

3 cut

Cut each of the fabric C squares in half vertically and horizontally to create a **total of (8)** 5" fabric C squares.

From the fabric F yardage, cut (1) 5" strip across the width of the fabric—subcut a **total of (8)** 5" fabric F squares.

4 make pinwheels

Place a fabric F square atop a fabric C square with right sides facing. Stitch around the outer edge using a ¼" seam allowance. Cut the square from corner to corner twice on the diagonal. Each sewn pair of squares will yield 4 half-square triangles. Open and press the seam allowance toward fabric C. Square each half-square triangle to 3". **4A**

Arrange 4 half-square triangles as shown. Sew the half-square triangles together in 2 rows. Press the seam of the top row to the left and the seam of the bottom row to the right. Nest the seams and sew the rows together to complete the block. Repeat with the remaining 5" squares to **make 8** Pinwheel Party blocks. **4B 4C**

Pinwheel Party Block Size: 5½" unfinished, 5" finished

Fabric Key

A	■	Dark Royal
B	■	Teal
C	■	Seafoam
D	■	Sunshine
E	■	Orange
F	□	White
G	■	Navy

Bound in Secrets and Lies

PART FIVE: PRESSING OUT THE SECRETS

a fiction novella, in six parts written by **Hillary Doan Sperry**

Jenny sat in her car parked in front of the little city hall building. Hamilton wasn't one of the lucky towns with a grand town square or big old clocks to remind people of when the town first started. Instead, they had a small, one-door firehouse that had been converted into the local City Hall and Chamber of Commerce. Finding out about the quilts that had sold so high in the auction seemed like a good distraction to keep her from investigating Grace's problems.

She'd spent the first part of her morning at the police station informing them about Jed and her conversation with the Reyeses and now she was here. Not thinking about thieves and houses and mysterious people that hurt women.

Jenny gripped the wheel, still wishing she could go follow up with the Reyeses or look into the bricks that Jed had used in both incidents. It's fine, she thought, normal people find out about normal things. I can do this. Jenny hoped to find out who had run the auction and how much the quilts had actually sold for. She'd barely stepped out of the car before Robert Holdin stormed out of the building.

He stopped when he saw her and asked, "What are you doing here?"

Jenny hadn't planned on having to verify her purpose. She smiled and gave a slight shrug. "Just checking on some quilt sales."

"Don't you have people at your company that do that?" He looked annoyed that she was in his territory. She hadn't even considered that he might be at the little city hall building.

"Are you the door guard?" She had meant it to be teasing, but he bristled and shoved past her.

"Mind your own business, Mrs. Doan." He pushed past her and started his car, peeling out of the parking space.

As his car squealed onto the main drag, Gretchen, the receptionist, ran out of the building waving a stack of papers in the air. "Wait!" she called after Robert's speeding car. Her hand dropped and her body sagged in defeat as she watched him go.

"Good morning, Gretchen." Jenny smiled, hoping she could brighten the woman's spirits. "How are you doing today?"

Gretchen let out a heavy breath. "He thinks he can do anything. Look at him speeding through town like the cops won't care."

Jenny looked back to the road but Robert was long gone. "Is that how your whole morning has gone?"

Gretchen looked at Jenny just noticing she was there. She forced a smile and tapped what looked like a stack of mail against her palm. "Not entirely. Robert was in taking care of some city ordinance issues. And then, with hardly any notice, he bolted out of the office and left a stack of junk mail on my desk like I'm his filing cabinet."

"Do you want some help?" Jenny asked, searching for a way to be of assistance. "I could take it to him."

Gretchen turned as if Jenny had handed her a gold prize. "Really? That is so sweet." She held the door open, letting Jenny through into the front office. "And what can I do for you?"

Jenny took the stack of mail from Gretchen. "I am checking in about the recent quilt auction. I want to know how things work for independent sales like that."

"Did you have a quilt in that crazy auction? I shouldn't be surprised. I mean, you're Jenny Doan." She laughed and started digging through a drawer next to her desk and pulled out a form. "I'm assuming you mean taxes and such. Of course, this is all informational since the auction house will handle that I assume, but this is all the current tax information for the county, and down here is Hamilton's info."

Jenny smiled and looked at the form like she understood it. Taxes were not what she had meant. "Whew! That's a lot. Some of those quilts were going so high. How much did they make at that thing? I was curious how mine did in comparison."

Gretchen leaned in as if excited to be sharing this bit of gossip. "You know, you're not the first person to ask me that. Charlie Reyes was in here first thing this morning asking about the auction. He told me that one of those quilts sold for almost $10,000. Can you imagine? Who knew quilting could be so lucrative?"

Jenny didn't have to fake her surprise. "Ten thousand?"

"Right!" Gretchen sat back in her chair. "I could make a lot of vests with that money."

Jenny looked over the woman's outfit. Her floral vest must have been handmade. Jenny clucked her tongue. "You didn't make this one, did you? Oh my goodness. You have a wealth of hidden talents."

Gretchen blushed, and Jenny tapped the counter trying to piece together what was off. There were some beautiful quilts out there, but a ten-thousand-dollar quilt would have been a big deal. There should have been marketing to get more buyers. In Jenny's work she would have known about it. Grace with her auction house would have known about it too.

Thinking of Grace, she remembered her last errand. She reached a hand toward Gretchen. "I have been helping Grace with her house since the fire, and she wanted to know if you could find out who'd been filing all those complaints. It's been so hard."

"I'm sure, and now with that land and imminent domain movement, I can imagine she's struggling. Here, let me pull the file. I know Robert's been working overtime with so many complaints these days but they'll settle down, I'm sure. These things come in waves."

"What imminent domain movement?" Jenny leaned forward, watching Gretchen pull the file and place it up on the counter.

"You don't know, do you? That's what Robert was in here working on this morning. I think he's going to talk to the homeowners. It's been proposed that it would be for the greater good of the community to seize several pieces of property that would then be sold to Merkle Fabrication. I don't believe it for a minute. Merkle would level the whole northeast corner of town just to put in pig farms."

"And that includes … Grace's property?" Jenny asked, suddenly on her toes.

Gretchen faltered as Jenny's tension spread between them. "Yes, well, I believe hers was the last piece. I think I have that in the notes from this morning's meeting. Would you like to see it too?"

Trying to keep control, Jenny nodded and sat back. "That would be nice. Thank you, Gretchen."

The older woman gave Jenny a look of trepidation and turned, seeking out another larger filing cabinet. Jenny looked down at the file she already had in front of her. City ordinance complaints hardly seemed to matter when they were going to take Grace's home anyway.

She flipped the file open, anxious to be doing something while Gretchen dug out the minutes from the meeting. Right on top was a complaint filed the day before by Charlie Reyes. Coming in two days in a row on a hurt leg didn't sound fun. He'd referenced his neighbor, Grace's property with four different citations marked on the sheet. Excess people on the property, junk in the yard, cars blocking the road, and a noise complaint.

None of it surprised Jenny, only adding to her frustration, until she noticed the time stamp—it was filed in early morning long before Grace had opened her doors. Even if Charlie had been up early, that only made the list of complaints look stranger.

Why would there have been a noise complaint or excess cars in the road before seven a.m.?

Jenny flipped the page, sick of looking at it. The next page was another land complaint against Grace—junk in the yard. She turned to the next one, and the next one. The top half of the stack were all repeated complaints against Grace. Below that were a handful of complaints against other people, all filed by Charlie Reyes. Every single one. Jenny flipped pages trying to remember what Charlie had said about Mish. He'd denied Mena being Mish but he never said he wasn't. And using Jed to injure himself was the perfect way to hide from prying eyes.

Jenny's mind spun as Gretchen set the minutes down in front of her. Jenny scanned the pages. There was nothing that she could see included about imminent domain, but Jenny didn't have time to search. If Charlie was after Grace, Jenny had to warn her. "Thank you so much. I'm going to hurry over to Grace's and see if I can catch Robert. Thank you for your time though. Would you mind if I took some photos of the documents in here? I don't need copies, I just want to remember a couple things to tell Grace."

Gretchen shrugged. "It's all public access. The city council has been very clear that they want these things to be transparent."

"Thank you." Jenny smiled and snapped a photo of several of the last complaints she'd looked at. "It was so nice to visit, Gretchen. Give a hug to those grandkids, and have a great day. I'll get these to Robert for you," Jenny added, holding up the stack of mail and making her way to the door.

Jenny did a quick scan of the mail as she stepped outside. It looked like preprinted flyers and insurance companies. It was no wonder he hadn't worried about taking it with him, but it had given her a reason to track Grace down. She opened the car door, and a gust of wind caught her by surprise. The mail flew from her grip and Jenny found herself chasing postcards about car washes.

She groaned as several pieces got away from her, and she grabbed the last of a stack of mail caught under the tire of a neighboring vehicle. Bidding good riddance to the pieces she'd missed, she ducked into her car. She dropped the mail into the passenger seat, the postcards splaying across the fabric cushion. Caught under several envelopes was a normal piece of notepaper that she hadn't noticed before, plainly printed with the header "Quilt Auction."

Jenny picked it up, looking over the list. It was printed quite differently than the way Grace handled her auctions, but if Charlie had been there talking about the auction that morning, this piece of paper could belong to him.

The page and the auction itself tugged at her. It still felt so odd that she'd heard nothing about it. If Charlie knew something, maybe she could go talk to him. It wasn't until she read the subheader that she stopped in her tracks. In tiny letters, it read, "Sponsored by Merkle Fabrications and Textiles."

"Merkle Fabrications," she muttered, flipping the page over. "Since when does an animal byproduct company take on textiles? Charlie, you know something, don't you?"

Still skimming the paper, Jenny reached down and turned on the engine. The flyer was printed double-sided and single-spaced with dozens of quilt names and patterns. She supposed the company could be trying to foster goodwill since they were forcing their way in, but as she looked over the long list, her gut told her a different story.

More than half of the listings were starred with large numbers penciled in the margins. Initially, she attributed the numbers to a product or listing number but several of them were the same. And when she found the quilt marked 9,875, she realized the numbers were dollar amounts. That was the quilt that had sold for nearly $10,000.

CONTINUED ON PAGE 102

Choosing Color with Confidence

What colors inspire you? Becoming more color aware is really about recognizing the ways that color inspires us every day and using that newfound sensibility in our personal quilting projects. Colors can have a strong effect on our emotions and can bring us comfort, joy, excitement, and peace. They can even spark conflict within ourselves. What colors remind you of places and things you love? Choosing colors with purpose can have a powerful effect.

Choosing colors for your quilting projects is a very personal experience. When you walk into a quilt shop, are there fabrics you immediately gravitate toward? Do you find yourself admiring a rainbow of solids? Do you dig patterns? Are you all about simple, bold designs? Or do you prefer to get lost in the details? There's always a place where you feel right at home. So, let's start there, in your comfort zone, and then see what possibilities lie beyond when you unlock the secrets of informed color choice.

Begin by looking around you. Search your surroundings and your treasured belongings. Open up your closet. Peruse old pictures. Take a walk around the neighborhood. Snap pictures, gather up memorabilia, and begin by creating a mood board. You can do this virtually, on Pinterest, or you can do it physically with swatches of fabric, scraps of paper, photographs, and magazine clippings. Either way, you'll start to get a sense of your personal style and the colors that excite and inspire you.

Once you have discovered the colors that bring you joy, they'll begin to jump out at you wherever you go, from the grocery store to the quilt shop. At this point, a trip to the paint store is in order! Indulge your love of color and pick up a bunch of color swatches you love. Bring them home and start arranging them in groups to create a palette for your next project!

As you work with color, here are a few considerations to help you explore greater possibilities. Learning to use color wisely is a skill that anyone can obtain. It begins with self-awareness and then moves into self-expression. Instead of choosing colors that are expected, you can embrace the unexpected with wonderful results!

Design with Purpose

When you're ready to take your quilt design to the next level, begin with hues you typically enjoy and dig a little deeper by asking these questions:

Does your design need high contrast areas or do you want a monochromatic look?

Do your color choices blend or stand out?

Where do you want the focus of the quilt to be—on the design, or on the fabric?

Do you want one or several colors to stand out?

Cut it Out
When you get your color card, it's absolutely beautiful, but not as useful as it might be. Don't be afraid to cut apart your color chips and create an organization system for yourself so you can easily mix and match colors. It's tough to see how colors interact with each other when they're stuck together. Another helpful tip is to take your individual color chips, mount them to magnets, and stick them on a magnetic white board for fast and fun color combinations!

The Color Wheel
The color wheel takes the basic three and breaks them down into three categories based on hue: primary, secondary, and tertiary. A color wheel becomes a powerful tool to explore greater possibilities when you use it to understand how complementary colors work together.

Primary Colors—Red, yellow, and blue are the three pigments that are mixed to create every other color. All other colors are formed from these three. They are the building blocks of color!

Secondary Colors—Orange, green, and purple are colors formed from mixing the primary colors in different combinations.

As quilters it can be overwhelming to know which colors to choose because there are just so many! Making color choices with a plan in mind provides boundaries that can encourage even greater creativity. Don't be afraid to take your color wheel along with you when you go to choose fabrics or pull it out at home when you're pulling fabrics from your stash.

Common Color Combinations

Monochromatic
Choosing one color and using variations of it exclusively.

Complementary
Choosing two colors that are directly opposite each other on the color wheel.

Spectrum
Using all of the colors on the wheel. A rainbow of possibilities!

Triadic
Choosing three colors that are evenly spaced around the color wheel, forming a triangle.

Analogous
Choosing a range of colors that are next to each other on the color wheel.

Color Value

Now that you understand how the color wheel works, it's time to talk about value. It's determined by how light or dark a color is. If you tend to choose colors that are medium value, not too light and not too dark, they are not going to create much contrast. To see the contrast in your design, squint at your fabrics. Another good way to determine value is to take a photo with your phone and turn it to grayscale or use the Ruby Ruler. Viewing your design on a design wall also helps quite a bit. Which fabrics stand out?

Choosing fabrics that are in different shades, tones, and tints change value. Pure colors are always going to stand out the most when compared to colors mixed with more gray, or tones. And yellow, when it's a pure color, is always going to stand out the most in any design, so keep that in mind. Warm colors in general are going to be more dominant than cool colors.

Shades—adding black to a color makes it darker.
Tones—adding gray to a color makes it more neutral.
Tints—adding white to a color makes it lighter.

This is where the color wheel comes in handy. You can use the color wheel to choose lower value colors or higher value colors depending on their placement on the wheel. Higher contrast comes when you combine complimentary colors that are directly across from each other on the wheel.

Color value also affects how colors respond to each other. For example, let's take red and contrast it with different color backgrounds. A pure red appears brighter against a black background and more subdued against a white background. Red also appears dulled when paired with orange, and brilliant when set against blue. In quilting, we are constantly juxtaposing fabrics of different colors. Take time to consider how those colors play off each other. Is it the the effect you want to achieve?

Is your quilt is feeling a bit flat even though it's crammed with color? You may think that simply increasing the contrast between your color values is the key to creating a design that has greater appeal, but it's not the only answer. That is part of it, but the other part is including value differences that are more subtle along with those stronger differences in contrast. Always pay attention to value as you piece together blocks to make your design sparkle!

JENNY'S JOURNAL

Peace in Pieces Quilt
by J. Michelle Watts

Back when I was a teenager, we didn't think twice about calling something groovy and flashing a cool peace sign. It's been years since I said the word groovy and meant it, and this quilt is definitely 'groovy'. Designed by J. Michelle Watts, *Peace in Pieces* is a quick jelly roll quilt that looks pretty impressive. I made this quilt especially for Missouri Star's 13th Birthday Bash because the theme was "Come Together" in honor of the peace-loving 1960s and it was auctioned off to benefit a local charity.

Pinehurst Quilt
by Edyta Sitar

When I saw this wintry quilt pattern by one of my favorite designers, Edyta Sitar, I knew I had to make it for the holiday season. So, I got together with my sewing buddy, Cherry, and we each created our own version. We're hoping to have enough holiday quilts made by December to do 12 days of Christmas porch quilts! Creating these little pine tree blocks was a lot of fun, we couldn't help but turn on some Christmas music while we stitched our quilts together.

A Bird that Sews Her Nest
Mini Missouri Star Quilt

The earth is filled with extraordinary creatures: Basilisk lizards can run on water, snails can nap for three full years, and there's a type of jellyfish that doesn't die—they grow old and then restart life as babies again and again and again. But perhaps most incredible of all is the tailorbird, for she can sew her own nest.

When a female tailorbird is ready to sew, she flits to a thick patch of foliage in search of the perfect leaf. It has to be healthy and malleable, with a nice, strong stem. (After all, every good sewing project begins with quality material.)

She wraps the leaf around her body to check the size. If it's a bit small, she'll gather another leaf or two and piece them together. She never uses pins; instead, she holds the leaves in place with her tiny feet, then pierces the seams with her needle-sharp beak.

Her thread is made of bits of cotton, lint, and cobwebs, which are carefully pushed through each little hole. Sometimes, a stitch pulls through or tears, but, like all good sewists, the tailorbird is not deterred by a few mistakes here and there. She takes the time to fix bad stitches and reinforce weak spots.

But let's be real: When the project seems to go up in smoke, she's not afraid to toss it aside and start fresh with a brand new leaf. She sews and she sews for two to four days, and when she's finished, her neat little nest boasts up to 200 stitches and looks like a cozy little cup made of leaves.

You may be wondering: What of the male? Where is he while the work is being done? He is busy gathering supplies! Like a dutiful husband carrying stacks of fabric bolts, the male tailorbird rushes here and there, bringing every needed scrap to his talented sweetheart.

When the sewing is done, a bit of leaf is bent to form a roof and provide shelter from tropical storms. The male tailorbird then hurries off to collect soft bits of grass, feathers, and fur to fill the nest and make it cozy.

Finally, when all is ready, his bride lays three to five blue, speckled eggs. For the next twelve days, she sits on the eggs and he brings the food, which sounds like a lovely arrangement to me.

When the babies hatch, Mr. and Mrs. Tailorbird cozy up together to care for those chickies in the safety of their very own, beak-stitched, home sweet home.

materials

QUILT SIZE
65" x 73"

BLOCK SIZE
8½" unfinished, 8" finished

QUILT TOP
1 package of 10" print squares
3½ yards of background fabric

BORDER
1¼ yards

BINDING
¾ yard

BACKING
4½ yards - vertical seam(s)
or 2¼ yards of 108" wide

OTHER
Clearly Perfect Slotted Trimmer A - optional

SAMPLE QUILT
Bohemian Blue by Lisa Audit for Wilmington Prints

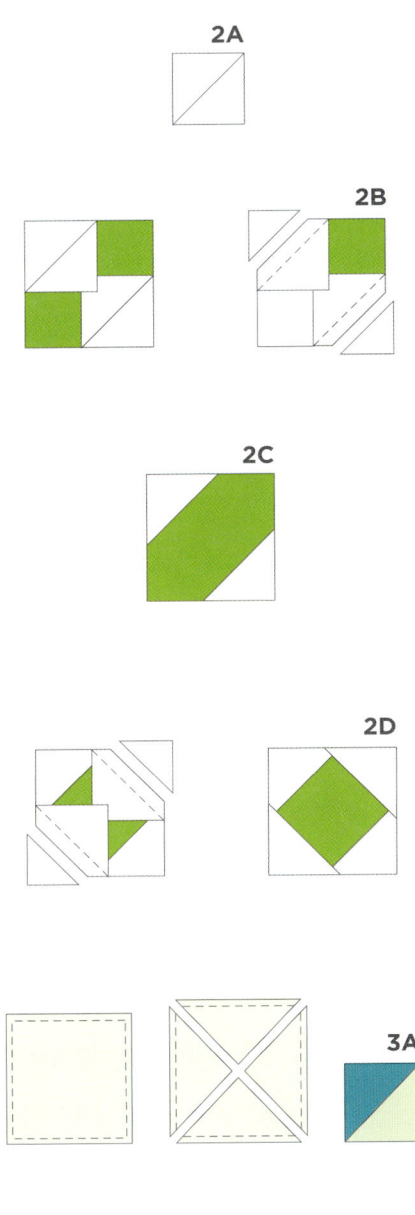

1 cut

Cut the 10" print squares in half horizontally and vertically to create (4) 5" squares from each. Trim a **total of 56** squares to 4½" for the star centers. You will have a **total of (112)** 5" squares remaining.

From the background fabric:
- Cut (16) 3" strips across the width of the fabric. Subcut a **total of (224)** 3" squares for section 3.

- Cut (28) 2½" strips across the width of the fabric. Subcut a **total of (448)** 2½" squares. Set aside 224 squares for section 2 and 224 squares for section 3.

2 make the center squares

Mark a diagonal line corner to corner on the reverse side of (224) 2½" background squares. **2A**

Lay a marked background square on 2 opposite corners of a 4½" print square as shown, right sides together. Sew along the marked lines, then trim the excess fabric ¼" away from the seam. **2B**

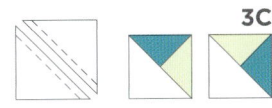

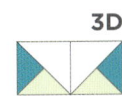

Press each snowballed corner over the seam. **2C**

Repeat to snowball the 2 remaining corners using 2 marked background squares. Square to 4½" if needed. **Make 56** center squares and set them aside for the moment. **2D**

3 block construction

Lay 2 unmatching 5" print squares 1 atop of the other, right sides facing. Sew around the perimeter. Cut the sewn squares twice diagonally. Open to reveal 4 half-square triangles. Press. Do not trim. **3A**

Draw a line from corner to corner once on the diagonal on the reverse side of each 3" background square. **3B**

Lay a marked 3" background square with a half-square triangle with the drawn line crossing over the seam of the half-square triangle. Sew ¼" away from the drawn line on both sides. Cut on the drawn line. If you are using the trimmer, lay your unit with the quarter-square triangle seam facing up. Match the centerline of the trimmer with the seam and trim each unit to 2½", then open and press. If you are not using the slotted trimmer, open each unit and press, then measure 1¼" from the center and trim to 2½" square. **Make 8**. **3C**

1. Mark a diagonal line on the reverse side of (224) 2½" background squares. Lay a marked square on 2 opposite corners of a 4½" print square as shown, right sides together. Sew along the marked lines, then trim the excess fabric ¼" away from the seam.

2. Press each snowballed corner over the seam. Repeat to snowball the 2 remaining corners using 2 marked background squares. Square to 4½" if needed. Make 56 center squares.

3. Lay 2 unmatching 5" print squares 1 atop of the other, right sides facing. Sew around the perimeter. Cut the sewn squares twice diagonally. Open to reveal 4 half-square triangles. Press. Do not trim.

4. Lay a marked square atop a half-square triangle with the line crossing the seam of the half-square triangle. Sew ¼" away from the line on both sides. Cut on the line. Trim to 2½". Make 8.

5. Sew 2 units together as shown. Notice the fabric placement is reflected in both units. Press. Make 4 star leg units.

6. Arrange (4) 2½" background squares, 4 star leg units, and a center square as shown. Sew the block together in rows. Press. Sew the rows together. Press. Make 56.

Sew 2 units together as shown. Notice the fabric placement is reflected in both units. Press. **Make 4** star leg units. **3D**

Arrange (4) 2½" background squares, 4 star leg units, and a center square as shown. **3E**

Sew the block together in rows. Press the top and bottom rows towards the background squares and the middle row towards the center square. Nest the seams and sew the rows together. Press. **Make 56**. **3F**

Block Size: 8½" unfinished, 8" finished

4 arrange & sew

Refer to the diagram on the left as necessary to lay out your blocks in **8 rows of 7**. Sew the blocks together in rows. Press the seams in opposite directions. Nest the seams and sew the rows together. Press.

5 border

Cut (7) 5" strips across the width of the border fabric. Sew the strips together to make 1 long strip. Trim the borders from this strip. Refer to Borders (pg. 118) in the Construction Basics to measure, cut, and attach the borders. The strip lengths are approximately 64½" for the sides and 65½" for the top and bottom.

6 quilt & bind

Layer the quilt with batting and backing, then quilt. See Construction Basics (pg. 118) to add binding and finish your quilt.

A Make-do Guy
Handy Dandy Quilt

The Handy Dandy quilt is based on a traditional 19th century quilt block called Handy Andy. It is named, of course, for the type of person who just "makes do."

You know the type: They can craft culinary delights from the meagerest of pantries. They can cultivate a blue-ribbon garden from rose bush cuts and the neighbors' extra lily bulbs. And, best of all, they can transform a pile of "useless" scraps into a beautiful quilted masterpiece.

Here at Missouri Star, our resident "Handy Andy" is none other than Jenny's cute husband, Ron Doan! Ron's limitless creativity combined with a knack for all-things mechanical make him a true master of all trades. And thank goodness for that! Their "happily ever after" would have never begun without Ron's penchant for fixin'!

You see, once upon a time, a lovely young Jenny Doan broke down in the church parking lot. Ron swooped in to fix the car and save the day. And the rest, as they say, is history!

Through the years, Ron has solved problems, mended breaks, and created a whole lot of fun for his family and friends. Alan, Ron and Jenny's oldest boy, says, "That's just Dad. He can do anything. He just figures out a way."

When the kids were young and money was tight, Ron and Jenny used plywood scraps to build a four-story dollhouse decked out with scads of tiny furniture. They primped and polished a second-hand bicycle until it was shiny and new. On Christmas morning, those hand made gifts were as beautiful and thrilling as anything from Santa's workshop.

One year at Halloween, Ron used his boundless talents to turn a big Victorian porch into a pirate ship, complete with cannons that fired flour "smoke." Another year he helped the grandkids craft Harry Potter magic wands.

He built a playhouse with a slide made of rollers from an old conveyor belt. He helped the boys construct their own tree forts, then attached a seventy-five foot zipline that stretched across the backyard. He even fashioned a little puppet theatre for the kids to put on puppet shows at the local library.

According to Jenny, "He is all-around amazing. He can fix any car or motorcycle, paint any room, and heal broken hearts with just a hug and a smile."

materials

QUILT SIZE
66" x 77"

BLOCK SIZE
10½" unfinished, 10" finished

QUILT TOP
1 roll of 2½" print strips*
  - includes piano key border
1 roll of 2½" background strips
1¼ yards of background fabric
  - includes sashing and
    inner border

BINDING
¾ yard

BACKING
4¾ yards - vertical seam(s)
  or 2½ yards of 108" wide

OTHER
Clearly Perfect Slotted Trimmers
  A & B

***Note**: The usable width of the print strips should be at least 43".

SAMPLE QUILT
Sew Fine Batiks by Kathy Engle
  for Island Batik

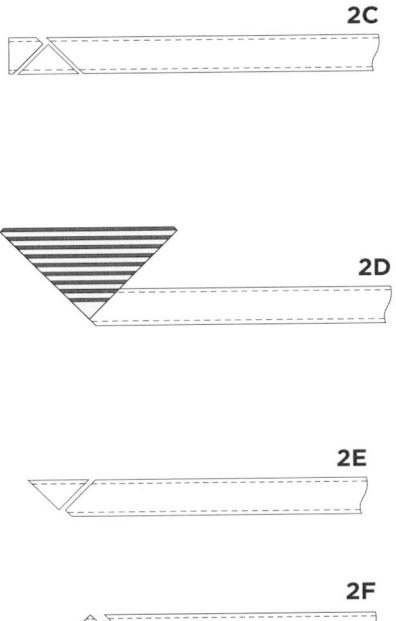

1 sort & cut

From the background fabric, cut:
- (2) 2½" strips across the width of the fabric. Add these to your roll of background strips.

- (24) 1½" strips across the width of the fabric.
  - Cut 8 strips into a **total of (30)** 1½" x 10½" sashing rectangles for section 5.
  - Cut 10 strips into a **total of (30)** 1½" x 11½" sashing rectangles for section 5.
  - Set 6 strips aside for the inner border.

From the roll of 2½" print strips:
- Select 10 light print strips and cut each into (8) 2½" x 5" rectangles for a **total of 80**.

- Keep each of the 30 remaining dark print strips folded in half. Cut a 5" increment from the loose ends of the folded strips, creating (2) 2½" x 5" rectangles from each for a **total of 60**.

- Set all of the 2½" x 5" rectangles aside for section 8 and the long dark print strips aside for section 2.

From the 2½" background strips:
- Select 30 strips and cut (3) 2½" squares from each. Set the 30 long strips aside for section 2.

- Select 11 strips and cut (16) 2½" squares from each strip.

- Select 1 strip and cut (4) 2½" squares. You will have a **total of (270)** 2½" background squares for section 4.

2 make the half-square triangles

Lay a 2½" background strip atop a 2½" dark print strip, right sides facing. Sew down both long edges creating a tube. **Make 30. 2A**

Lay a strip set on your cutting surface. Lay trimmer A on the strip set, lining up the 2½" mark of the trimmer with the bottom seam of the tube and the left edge of the tube. **2B**

Cut along the right edge of the trimmer first. Move the strip set out of the way, then cut along the left side of the trimmer. **Note**: If you are left-handed, you may prefer to reverse these directions and start trimming from the right end of the tube. **2C**

1. Lay a 2½" background strip atop a 2½" dark print strip, right sides facing. Sew down both long edges creating a tube. Lay trimmer A on the strip set, lining up the 2½" mark of the trimmer with the bottom seam of the tube and the left edge of the tube.

2. Cut along the right edge of the trimmer first. Move the strip set out of the way, then cut along the left side of the trimmer.

3. Turn the trimmer 180° and line up the 2½" mark of the trimmer with the top edge of the strip set. Cut along the right edge of the trimmer.

4. Use Trimmer B to cut (4) 3" units from the same tube. Open and press. Repeat to make 30 sets of 12 matching 2½" half-square triangles and to make 30 sets of 4 matching 3" half-square triangles.

5. Draw a diagonal line, across the sewn seam, on the reverse side of a 3" half-square triangle. Lay the marked unit atop another, right sides facing, and backgrounds touching prints. Sew on both sides of the line. Cut on the line. Press. Trim each unit to 2½". Make 30 sets of 4.

6. Select 1 set of half-square triangles, 1 set of hourglass units, and (9) 2½" background squares. Arrange the units in 5 rows of 5 as shown. Sew the units together in rows. Press in opposite directions. Sew the rows together. Press. Make 30.

Turn the trimmer 180° and line up the 2½" mark of the trimmer with the top edge of the strip set. Cut along the right edge of the trimmer. **2D 2E**

Turn the trimmer 180° again and line up the 2½" mark of the trimmer with the bottom seam of the tube. You will need to cut along the right edge of the trimmer, followed by the left edge as you did previously. **2F**

Continue in this manner to cut (12) 2½" units from the tube, each time trimming the extra small strip when the trimmer is aligned along the bottom edge.

Repeat the cutting instructions, this time using Trimmer B, to cut (4) 3" units from the same tube. Open and press each unit. Repeat with each tube to **make 30** sets of 12 matching 2½" half-square triangles and to **make 30** sets of 4 matching 3" half-square triangles. Set aside the 2½" units for section 4 and the 3" units for section 3. **2G**

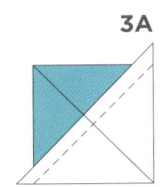

3 make the hourglass units

Draw a line on the diagonal, perpendicular to the sewn seam, on the reverse side of a 3" half-square triangle. **3A**

Lay the marked half-square triangle atop another matching half-square triangle, right sides facing, and background halves touching print halves. Sew ¼" away from the drawn line on both sides. Cut on the drawn line. Match the centerline of the trimmer with the seam and trim each unit to 2½", then open and press. Repeat with the remaining half-square triangles to **make 30** sets of 4 matching hourglass units. **3B**

4 block construction

Select 1 set of half-square triangles, 1 set of hourglass units, and (9) 2½" background squares. The prints in each set should differ. Arrange the units in 5 rows of 5 as shown. **4A**

Sew the units together in rows. Press the seams in opposite directions. Nest the seams and sew the rows together. Press. **Make 30**. **4B**

Block Size: 10½" unfinished, 10" finished

5 add sashing

Sew a 1½" x 10½" sashing rectangle to the bottom of a block. Press towards the rectangle. Sew a 1½" x 11½" sashing rectangle to the left side of the unit just sewn. Press towards the rectangle. **Make 30**. **5A**

6 arrange & sew

Refer to the diagram on the next page as necessary to lay out your units in **6 rows of 5 sashed blocks**. Notice how the sashing of each block is rotated in the diagram. Sew the blocks together in rows. Press the seams in opposite directions. Nest the seams and sew the rows together. Press.

7 inner border

Sew the (6) 1½" strips together to make 1 long strip. Trim the borders from this strip. Refer to Borders (pg. 118) in the Construction Basics to measure, cut, and attach the borders. **Note**: The top and bottom borders were attached first for this quilt. The strip lengths are approximately 55½" for the top and bottom and 68½" for the sides.

8 piano key border

Refer to Borders (pg. 118) in the Construction Basics to measure the length of your quilt top and make any adjustments necessary while sewing the pieced border. The sides of your quilt should measure approximately 68½".

4A

4B

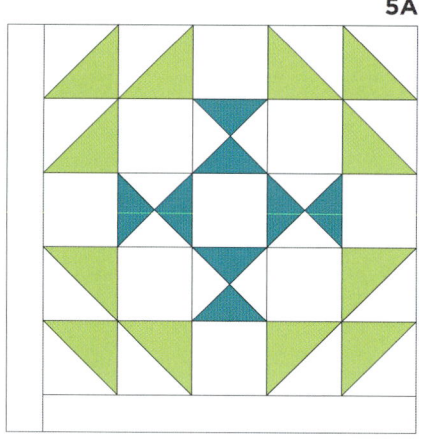

5A

Arrange (35) 5" print strips, alternating from light and dark prints. **Note**: We used (35) 5" print strips on our quilt but you may only need 34 depending on the width of your seams. You may also need to use some of your darkest light prints as dark prints. Sew the units together to form a border strip, making any adjustments to the seam allowances necessary to match the length of your quilt. **Make 2** piano key side border strips.

Refer to Borders (pg. 118) in the Construction Basics to attach 1 border to either side of your quilt top.

Measure the width of your quilt top as you did before. If needed, make any adjustments to the border. The quilt top width should measure approximately 66½". Arrange (33) 5" print strips, alternating from light and dark prints. Sew the units together to form a border strip. **Make 2** piano key border strips.

Refer to Borders (pg. 118) in the Construction Basics to attach these borders to the top and bottom of your quilt top.

9 quilt & bind

Layer the quilt with batting and backing, then quilt. See Construction Basics (pg. 118) to add binding and finish your quilt.

Spice Up Your Life
Radiant Reindeer Wall Hanging

It won't be long before October arrives and things start to get "spicy." Which autumn treat are you looking forward to the most? We're already counting down the days until every drink, pastry, candle, and perfume is infused with pumpkin spice and cinnamon! Speaking of this delicious duo, have you ever noticed cinnamon tends to get overshadowed by pumpkin spice? If you fancy yourself a spice specialist, you probably see the irony in this, considering cinnamon is the main ingredient for pumpkin spice. Without the warm, sweet, and tingly delight of cinnamon, there would be no pumpkin pie to smother in whipped cream or pumpkin spice lattes to sip until winter's end! But the irony of cinnamon doesn't stop there, it actually began in a few warmer regions of the world.

Now, you're probably wondering how a spice that is a staple flavor for autumn and winter could have originated anywhere without snow or colorful leaves. Cinnamon, or cinnamomum verum (oof, try saying that three times fast!) is actually native to India, Sri Lanka, Bangladesh, and Myanmar. Made from the bark of the cinnamon tree, "true cinnamon," is a decadent spice that has been used for various purposes for thousands of years! It was often used during embalming processes in ancient Egypt, and apparently for scenting anointing oil in the Old Testament. Over the centuries, it became one if not the most luxurious spice traded in the sea spice routes between India and China, and it's believed to be what encouraged European explorers to venture out to Asia and the other "spice islands."

Cinnamon is still very much treasured today, and we don't have to cross the ocean to buy it! The Asia-Pacific area remains the world's leading producer of cinnamon, with Indonesia being the largest supplier. It's still obtained through cinnamon trees, and you've probably seen it sold as delicate sticks (also called "quills") or finely ground reddish-brown powder.

Did you know that there are actually two main types of spice labeled as "cinnamon," and the one most commonly used in the U.S. and the U.K. is called "cassia"? Yep! Cinnamonum cassia is the other species of this delicious spice. In fact, in the U.K. and several other countries, cassia must be labeled and sold as "cassia," never "cinnamon." As far as we're concerned, it can have as many names as it wants as long as it continues to spice up our drinks, pastries, and pies, and makes the cold seasons a little warmer!

materials

PROJECT SIZE
20" x 39¼"

REINDEER SIZE
6¾" x 6¾" finished

PROJECT SUPPLIES
¼ yard white fabric
1 yard brown fabric
¾ yard print fabric
2 Rainbow Classic 9" x 12"
  Felt Squares - Black
¼ yard Heat n Bond Lite*
1 package of Missouri Star
  Quilter's Best Blend Crib Batting
(3) 2" x 40" fusible fleece strips
⅝" x 24" dowel

Basting spray - recommended
6 yards medium weight red yarn
  for Rudolph's nose - optional*
Missouri Star Circle Magic Large
  5" Circle Template - optional

*A scrap of red fabric can be substituted for the yarn on Rudolph's nose.

SAMPLE PROJECT
Hay... It's Christmas - Red Plaid
  by Russell Cobane for Northcott,
Kona Cotton Chocolate and White
  by Robert Kaufman Fabrics

1 cut

Find the templates at **msqc.co/radiant-reindeer** and print 1 copy. Cut out each paper template along the darkest outline.

From the white fabric, cut (3) 2¾" strips across the width of the fabric.

From the brown fabric:
- Cut (4) 5" strips across the width of the fabric. Use the circle template and subcut a **total of 18** circles.

- From the remaining fabric, use the outer ear template to trace and cut a **total of 36** outer ears.

From the print fabric, cut (6) 2½" strips across the width of the fabric. Trim each strip to 2½" x 40½".

From the black felt squares:
- Use the antler template to trace and cut a **total of 18**.

- Use the nose template to trace and cut a **total of 8**.

From the Heat n Bond Lite:
- Cut (3) 2½" strips across the width of the fusible.

- Cut (1) 4¾" strip across the width of the fusible. Subcut (2) 4¾" squares.

From the batting:
- Cut (1) 5" strip across the width of the batting. Use the circle template to trace 9 batting circles, then cut ¼" inside the drawn line.

- Cut (1) 1½" strip across the width of the batting. Use the outer ear template to trace 18 outer ears, then cut ¼" inside the drawn curved line only. (Trim on the straight edge of the drawn line.)

2 trace, fuse, & cut

Use the templates to trace 18 inner ears and 9 muzzles on the paper side of the 2½" Heat n Bond strips. Follow the manufacturer's directions to adhere the fusible strips to the reverse side of the 2¾" white strips. Cut out each piece and remove the paper backing.

Note: If you choose to use a scrap of red fabric for Rudolph's nose, repeat the directions to trace, fuse, and cut 1 red nose.

3 appliqué

Arrange an inner ear piece atop an outer ear as shown. Both pieces should be right side up. Follow the manufacturer's instructions to fuse the inner ear to the outer ear. Appliqué around the edge of the inner ear using a zigzag or blanket stitch. **Make 18**. **3A**

1. Arrange an inner ear piece atop an outer ear as shown right side up. Fuse the inner ear to the outer ear. Appliqué around the edge of the inner ear using a zigzag or blanket stitch. Make 18.

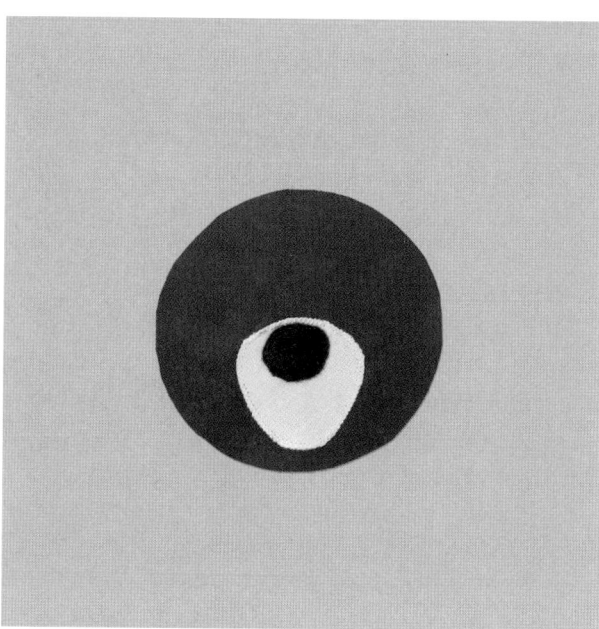

2. For a regular reindeer, arrange the black nose atop the muzzle, as shown, and use basting spray or pins to hold in place. Appliqué around the muzzle and nose.

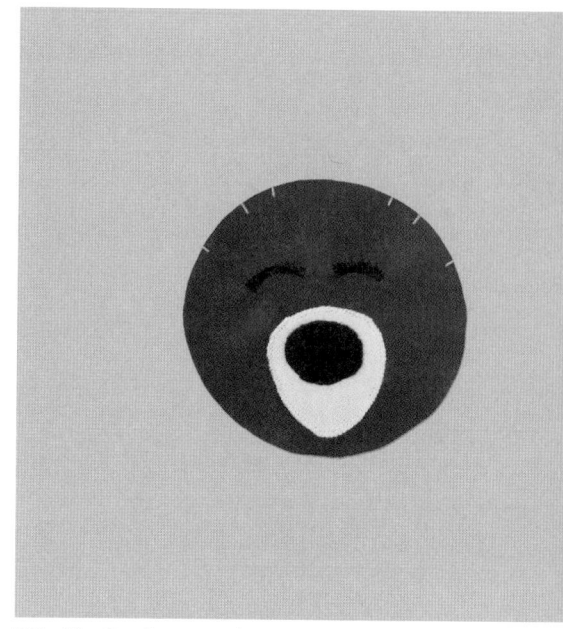

3. Use the face template to mark the eyes. Zigzag atop your marked lines, backstitching at both ends. Press over the eyes being careful not to press the felt nose. Use the face template to mark the placement of each antler and ear. Make 9.

4. Arrange the ears and antlers atop the face within the marks you just made as shown. Pin in place. Pin the antlers down away from the circle's edge to prevent them from being caught in the seam. Baste the ears and antlers to the face using a ⅛" seam allowance.

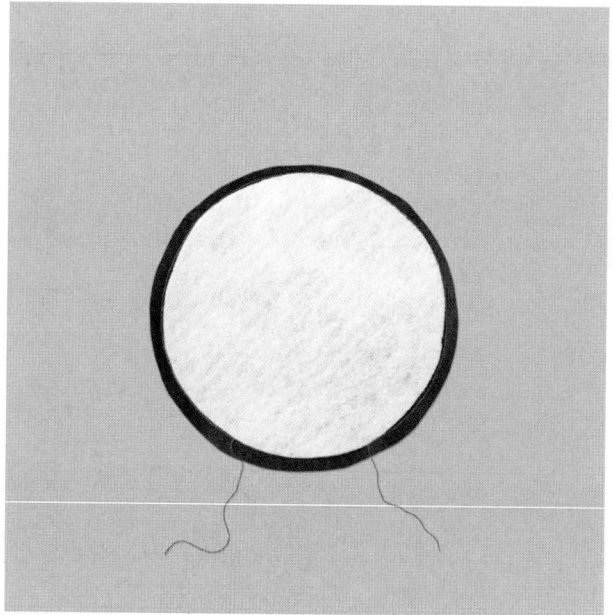

5. Leaving the pin that holds the antlers out of the way, lay the face, right sides together, atop the second brown circle. Pin as needed. Sew around the circle using a ¼" seam allowance and leave a 3" gap for turning along the bottom.

6. Clip the curve and turn right sides out. Remove the pin holding the antlers. Push out the edges to smooth the circle and press. Fold the edges of the 3" gap in ¼" and whipstitch the opening closed. Make 9.

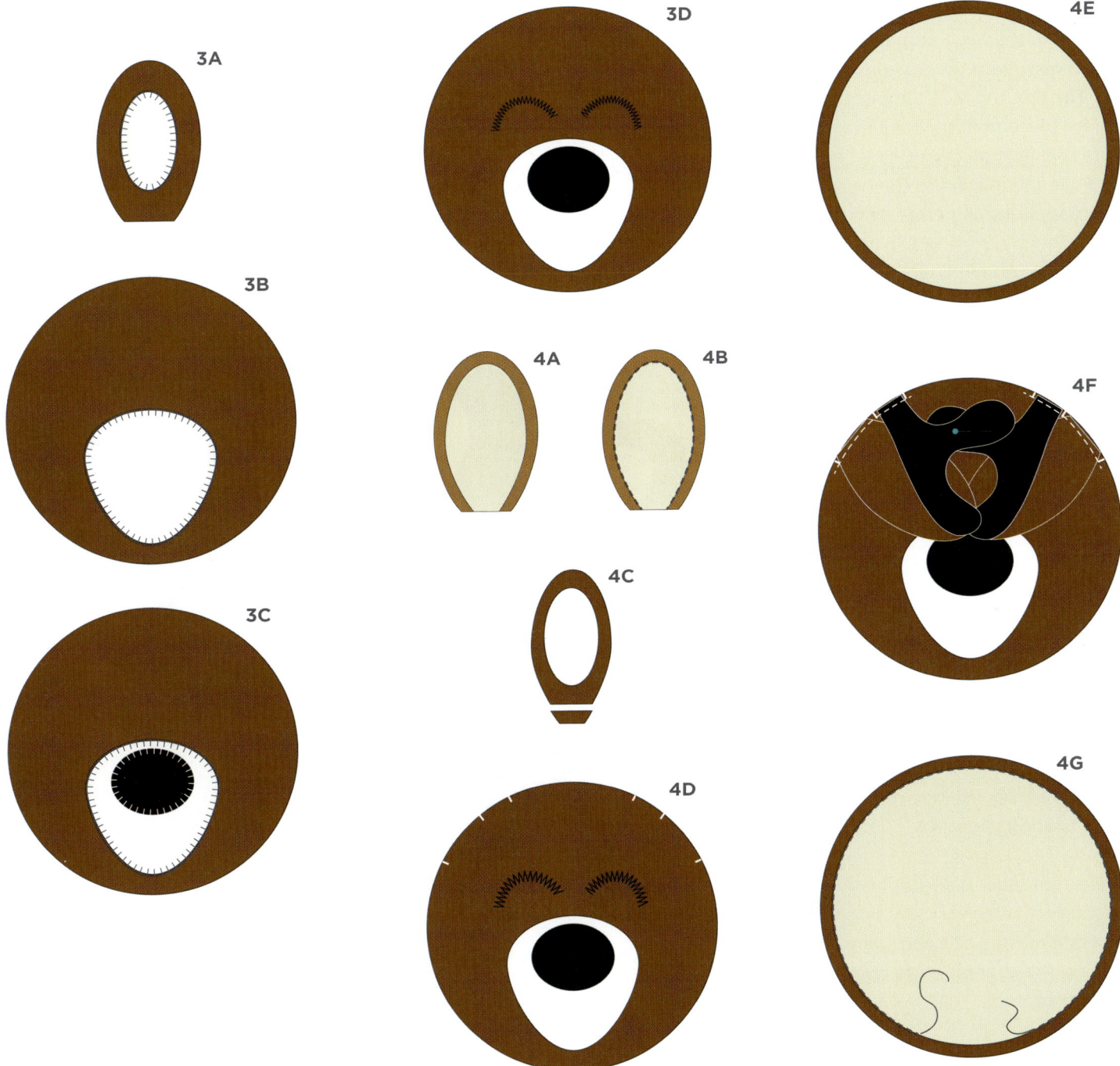

Radiant Reindeer Wall Hanging

Arrange a muzzle piece atop a brown circle as shown, with both pieces right side up. **Tip**: Use the face template as a guide for placement by holding the template and face pieces up to a light source. Fuse the muzzle to the brown circle and appliqué as before. **Make 9**. **3B**

For a regular reindeer, arrange the black nose atop the muzzle, as shown, and use basting spray or pins to hold in place. Appliqué around the nose. **Make 8**. **3C**

Note: For Rudolph, adhere the red fabric nose or add a red pom-pom nose later.

Use the face template on a light source again to line up the muzzle and nose, then mark the eyes. Zigzag atop your marked lines, backstitching at both ends. Press over the eyes being careful not to press the felt nose. **Make 9**. **3D**

4 reindeer construction

Adhere a batting ear piece to the reverse side of each appliquéd inner/outer ear using the basting spray. **4A**

Lay 1 inner/outer ear piece, right sides facing, atop an outer ear. Sew along the curved edge using a ¼" seam allowance and leaving the straight edge open for turning. **4B**

4H

5A

5B

Clip the curve and turn right sides out. Press. Trim ¼″ off the straight edge of the ear. **Make 18** ears. **4C**

Use the face template to mark the placement of each antler and ear. **Tip**: Make your marks along the circle's edge less than ¼″. **4D**

Adhere a batting circle to the reverse side of a face circle using the basting spray. **4E**

Arrange the ears and antlers atop the face within the marks you just made. Notice that the inner portions of the ears are face down and the raw edges are matched. The straighter side of each antler should be next to the ear. Pin in place. Pin the antlers down away from the circle's edge to prevent them from being caught in the seam. Baste the ears and antlers to the face using a ⅛″ seam allowance. **4F**

Leaving the pin that holds the antlers out of the way, lay the face, right sides together, atop the second brown circle. Pin as needed. Sew around the circle using a ¼″ seam allowance and leave a 3″ gap for turning along the bottom. **4G**

Clip the curve and turn right sides out. Remove the pin holding the antlers. Push out the edges to smooth the circle and press. Fold the edges of the 3″ gap in ¼″ and whipstitch the opening closed. **Make 9**. **4H**

Radiant Reindeer Wall Hanging

5 optional Rudolph nose

From the 6 yards of red yarn, cut a 10" segment. Wrap the remaining yarn around 2 fingers until you come to the end of the yarn. Carefully slide the yarn off your fingers, keeping the yarn in it's loop formation. Use the 10" segment to tightly tie a knot around the center of the loops as shown. **5A**

Fluff the yarn, then trim the pom-pom round to approximately 1½". Attach the pom-pom as Rudolph's nose by hand. **5B**

6 string your reindeer

Lay (2) 2½" x 40½" print strips right sides together. Lay a 2½" fusible fleece strip, glue side down, on the reverse side of the strips. Center the fusible strip as shown. Follow the manufacturer's directions to adhere the fleece to the print strip. **6A**

Measure and mark the center of 1 short end of the strips. Measure and mark 2" from the same end, up both sides. **6B**

Mark a line from the center mark to the 2" mark on both sides. Cut on the lines. **6C**

Sew a ¼" along the edges of the strips, leaving the short straight end open for turning. **6D**

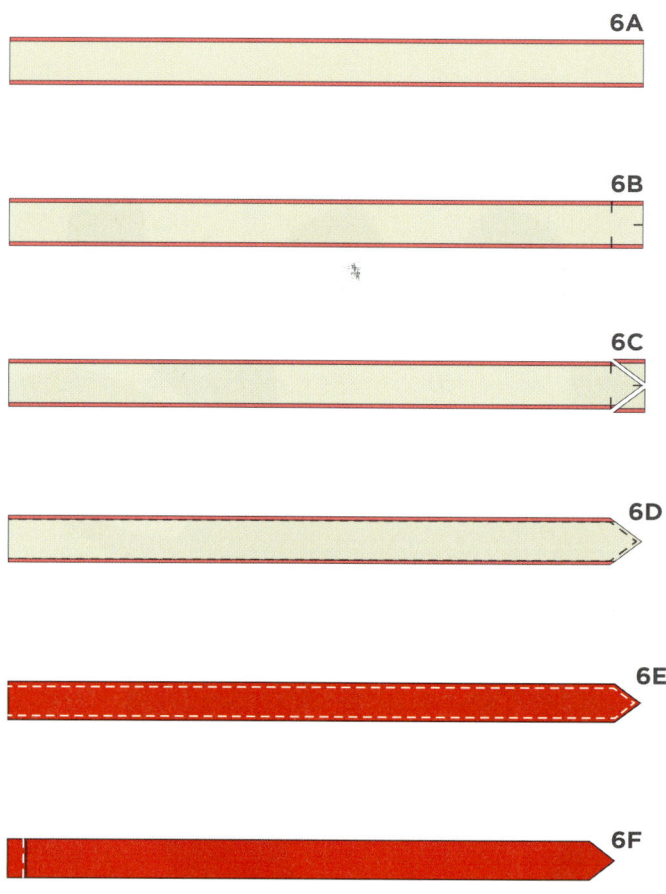

Clip the point and turn right sides out. Press. Topstitch ⅛" around the long edges and pointed end. **6E**

Fold the straight raw edge over ¼" and press. Fold over another 1" and topstitch along the fold to secure. Repeat to **make 3**. **6F**

Arrange the reindeer as shown in the diagram on the left. Attach the reindeer by hand or hot glue. **Tip**: Lightly attach the antlers to keep them from becoming floppy. Measure the width of the three ribbons of reindeer and add 4" to your width. Trim the dowel to this measurement, approximately 20". Slide the dowel rod through the loops at the top of each fabric strip and secure with hot glue. Hang your Radiant Reindeer and welcome Santa to your home!

CONTINUED FROM PAGE 69

She had a sense of awe looking at it. She started roughly calculating the numbers, but stopped when she hit over $100,000 without making it through the first page. In the margin on the opposite side of the page, written in small letters, were tiny names: Samuel, Lincoln, Ritchie—but it was Prairie that stopped her this time. She didn't know anyone named Prairie, but Grace's home was on Prairie Street.

Jenny flipped open her phone. The photo app was still open and right on top was a complaint for Grace's home on Prairie Street. She flipped to the next one, a house on Lincoln. It was the only complaint for that house if she remembered right. Then, two houses on Ritchie Street and one on Samuel Street. The last had multiple complaints as well. She looked at the auction sheet. Jenny didn't know what these had to do with each other, but Charlie Reyes might be the missing piece to the puzzle.

Jenny pulled out her phone and dialed Cherry's number.

"Good morning, my friend," she answered cheerily.

"Cherry, I need you to meet me at Grace's."

***

Cherry's car was already in the driveway as Jenny pulled up to Grace's home. She parked next to the same car that had peeled out of city hall's parking lot that morning. Robert Holdin stood on Grace's porch, handing a piece of paper to a tearful Grace.

Both women hurried from the vehicle in time to pass the far too cheerful man. Cherry acknowledged him, nodding her head and giving a steely, "Commissioner." Jenny went straight up the stairs to Grace.

"Are you okay?" Jenny asked as tears streamed down Grace's face.

She wiped at them fruitlessly and shook her head. "They want my house."

Jenny was a fixer, and while she'd started running scenarios through her head, it was Cherry who reached out first. She made it up the steps and wrapped Grace in a hug before Jenny realized she was still processing clues. It was how she lived, how she quilted. She solved problems. Every time she flipped a block around, it created a new pattern and Jenny was busy flipping blocks around in her head when she realized she was making a lot of assumptions.

"What did he say? It's not imminent domain, is it?" Jenny asked.

Grace's tears hid the confusion of her response, muffled through Cherry's blouse. "How did you know?" She held out the page. "He says I have a week and I have to be gone."

"Robert is out of line. We'll fight this, Grace."

She shook her head. "It's worse than that. Do you remember telling me to put the deed to my house in a safe? Well, I went to go get it last night and it's gone. I don't know what happened but it's gone. We can't fight it. I won't even be able to stay the week."

"That's not possible. Jed wouldn't do that."
Jenny was dumbfounded.

Cherry put her arm around Grace and they went inside.

Jenny's brain flipped those quilt blocks around furiously, but every way she tried, nothing fit. She felt like she'd failed Grace.

Jenny dropped to the porch. She tried to look over the document but all she could see was the burned shell of Grace's life. From this angle, she could see straight through the charcoaled corner of the barn to the missing section of roof. It was all that Grace had left and they were going to take even that.

Jenny looked down at the page signed by Commissioner Robert Holdin and tried not to be angry with him. Across the yard, the Reyes's home peeked out around Grace's place. Something or someone had moved and caught her attention. Charlie and Mena were loading quilts into their car.

That doesn't feel right, Jenny thought. Where are they taking those quilts?

The Reyeses went inside, and Jenny hurried across the grass, glancing behind her. Grace and Cherry were fine. Pausing at the large bushes that separated the properties, she'd have to pass the house to get to the car. It was a risk and just before moving out into the open, Jenny heard voices.

"This is it, right?" It was Mena's question, and Jenny could almost feel the nerves in it. Whatever was going down, Charlie and Mena were neck deep.

"Their money's already gone. So yeah, this is the final step. Once they have the land rights, we can walk away with everything we want."

"I don't want the money anymore." All motion stopped at Mena's announcement.

"Babe, this is why we're here. It's for our family. In Vitro is expensive."

"I know, but so is prison. I want to live in our little house and take care of you because you need me, not because you're a part of a crime ring and you've been hurt again."

Jenny had to focus on keeping her breathing slow and quiet as the Reyeses took their conversation inside. She ran over to their car. Sure enough, the quilts Mena had been binding were inside. She opened the door, noticing that several of the quilts, if not all, had a section of white binding like Mena had used to "repair"

Grace's quilt. Jenny ran a hand over the fabric noticing a stiffness in that section of the quilt. It could be the proof she needed.

In the front seat someone had tucked a basket of sewing essentials. Quietly, Jenny opened the front door and removed a pair of scissors from the basket. Jenny shot a glance at the house before going to work, removing that section of the binding.

"Jenny!" Cherry called from somewhere across the yard. "Jenny, are you still out here?"

Jenny glanced toward Cherry's voice and wished she could tell her to stay quiet. When she turned back, Mena Reyes was standing on the porch, her eyes locked on Jenny.

to be continued...

Reference

Streamer Quilt As You Go

designed by Laura Piland

QUILT SIZE
92" x 92"

BLOCK SIZE
58½" unfinished, 58" finished

QUILT TOP
6 different fabrics are needed for the star & pieced borders
- Fabric A - ½ yard
- Fabric B - ¾ yard
- Fabric C - 1 yard
- Fabric D - 1 yard
- Fabric E - 1¼ yards
- Fabric F - 1 yard

4½ yards background fabric
   - includes borders

BINDING
¾ yard

BACKING
8½ yards - vertical seam(s)
   or 2¾ yards of 108" wide

SAMPLE QUILT
Beside the Sea by Makower UK for Andover Fabrics

PATTERN
P. 12

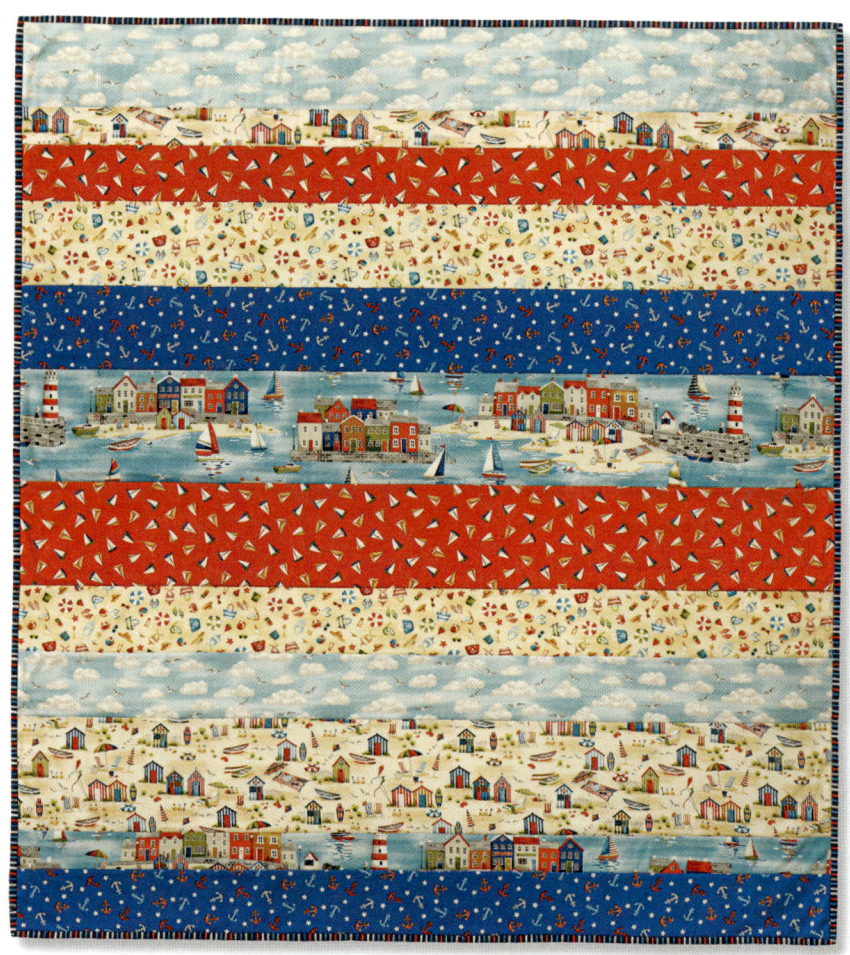

Seeing Double

QUILT SIZE
59" x 75"

BLOCK SIZE
16½" unfinished, 16" finished

QUILT TOP
1 package of 10" print squares
3 yards of background fabric

BORDER
1¼ yards

BINDING
¾ yard

BACKING
3¾ yards - horizontal seam(s)

OTHER
Clearly Perfect Slotted
 Trimmer A - optional

SAMPLE QUILT
Jungle Paradise by Stacy Iest Hsu
 for Moda Fabrics

QUILTING PATTERN
Froggie

PATTERN
P. 18

Supernova

QUILT SIZE
49½" x 60½"

BLOCK SIZE
6" unfinished, 5½" finished

QUILT TOP
1 package of 10" print squares
2¼ yards of background fabric

BINDING
½ yard

BACKING
3¼ yards - horizontal seam(s)

OTHER
Clearly Perfect Slotted Trimmer B
  - optional

SAMPLE QUILT
Sunprint by Alison Glass
  for Andover Fabric

QUILTING PATTERN
Champagne Bubbles

PATTERN
P. 26

Playground

QUILT SIZE
59" x 59"

BLOCK SIZE
12½" unfinished, 12" finished

QUILT TOP
1 package 10" print squares
1 roll of 2½" background strips

BORDER
1¼ yards

BINDING
¾ yard

BACKING
3¾ yards - horizontal seam(s)

SAMPLE QUILT
Artisan Batiks Evening Glow
   by Lunn Studios for Robert Kaufman

QUILTING PATTERN
Free Swirls

PATTERN
P. 38

Pinwheel Frolic

QUILT SIZE
65" x 65"

BLOCK SIZE
10½" unfinished, 10" finished

QUILT TOP
2 packages of 5" print squares
2 packages of 5" background squares

INNER BORDER
½ yard

OUTER BORDER
1¼ yards

BINDING
¾ yard

BACKING
4¼ yards - vertical seam(s) or 2¼ yards of 108" wide

SAMPLE QUILT
Summer Breeze
by Moda Fabrics

QUILTING PATTERN
Brocade Fans

PATTERN
P. 46

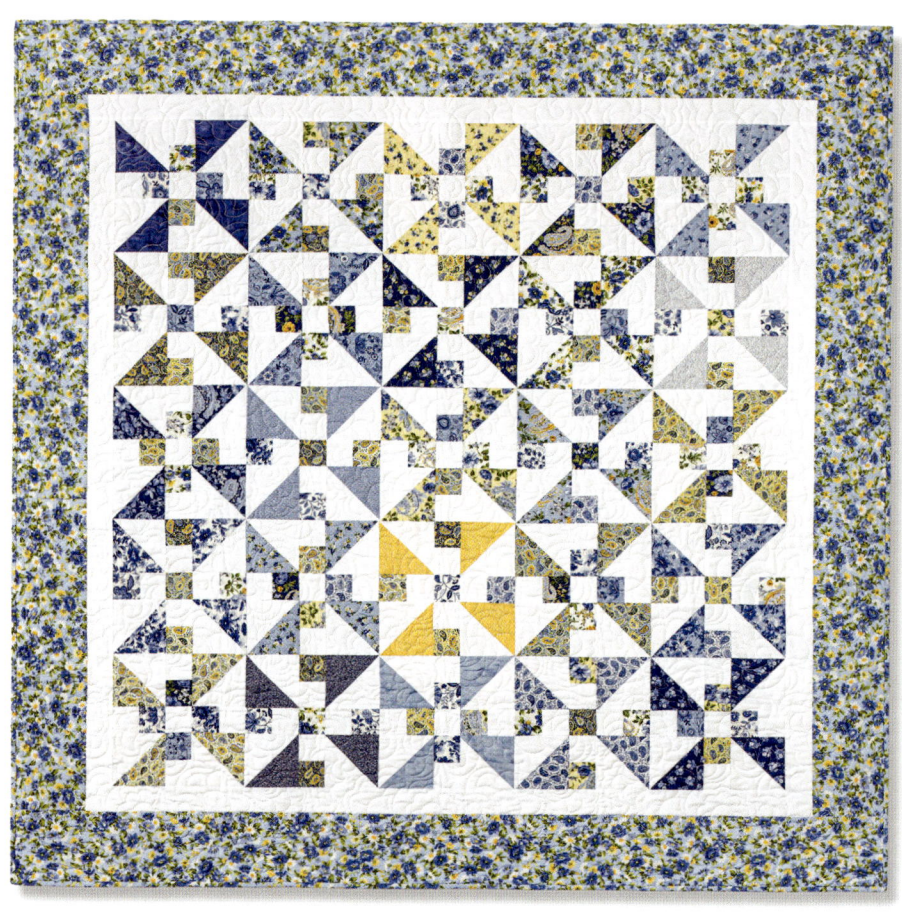

Goose Tracks

QUILT SIZE
73" x 73"

BLOCK SIZE
18½" unfinished, 18" finished

QUILT TOP
3 packages of 5" print squares
1½ yards of background fabric
 - includes inner border

OUTER BORDER
1¾ yards

BINDING
1 yard

BACKING
4½ yards - vertical seam(s)
 or 2¼ yards of 108" wide

OTHER
Scallops, Vines & Waves
 Template for Quilt in a Day®
The Bias Binding Tool
 for TQM Products

SAMPLE QUILT
Bluebird by Edyta Sitar
 of Laundry Basket Quilts
 for Andover Fabric

QUILTING PATTERN
Circle Meander

PATTERN
P. 52

Breezy Windmills

QUILT SIZE
85" x 93"

BLOCK SIZE
8½" unfinished, 8" finished

QUILT TOP
1 roll of 2½" print strips
1 roll of 2½" background strips

INNER BORDER
¾ yard

OUTER BORDER
1½ yards

BINDING
¾ yard

BACKING
8½ yards - vertical seam(s)
or 3 yards of 108" wide

SAMPLE QUILT
Prairie Dreams
by Kansas Troubles Quilters
for Moda Fabrics

QUILTING PATTERN
Simple Stipple

PATTERN
P. 58

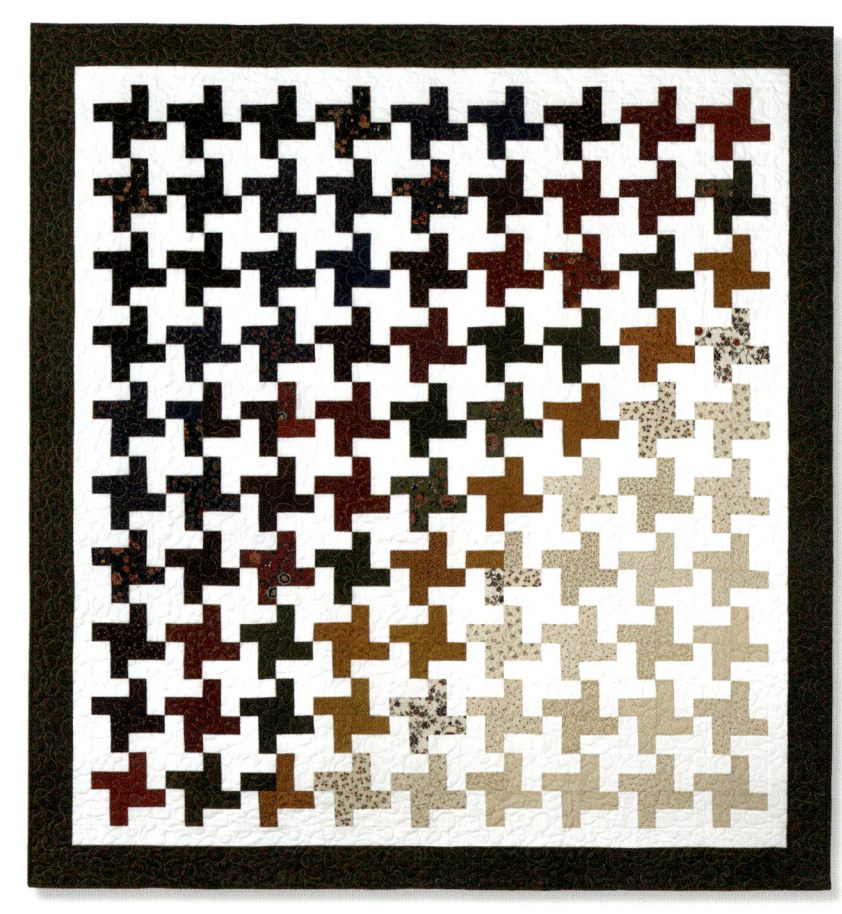

SUPER EASY HOURGLASS

PINWHEEL PARTY

Talavera Tile

Super Easy Hourglass + Pinwheel Party
(Blocks Only)

SUPER EASY HOURGLASS BLOCK SIZE
6¼" unfinished, 5¾" finished

PINWHEEL PARTY BLOCK SIZE
5½" unfinished, 5" finished

BLOCK SUPPLIES - SUPER EASY HOURGLASS
(2) 10" fabric D squares
(2) 10" fabric E squares

BLOCK SUPPLIES - FANCY FLIGHT
(2) 10" fabric C squares
(1) 5" fabric F strip - cut from yardage

Note: *Fabrics A, B, and G are not used in Part 5.*

SAMPLE QUILT
Circle Burst Wilmington Essentials
   by Wilmington Prints
Vintage Texture Wilmington Essentials
   by Wilmington Prints

QUILTING PATTERN
Free Swirls

PATTERN
P. 64

Mini Missouri Star

QUILT SIZE
65" x 73"

BLOCK SIZE
8½" unfinished, 8" finished

QUILT TOP
1 package of 10" print squares
3½ yards of background fabric

BORDER
1¼ yards

BINDING
¾ yard

BACKING
4½ yards - vertical seam(s)
  or 2¼ yards of 108" wide

OTHER
Clearly Perfect Slotted
  Trimmer A - optional

SAMPLE QUILT
Bohemian Blue by Lisa Audit
  for Wilmington Prints

QUILTING PATTERN
Variety

PATTERN
P. 78

Handy Dandy

QUILT SIZE
66" x 77"

BLOCK SIZE
10½" unfinished, 10" finished

QUILT TOP
1 roll of 2½" print strips*
  - includes piano key border
1 roll of 2½" background strips
1¼ yards of background fabric
  - includes sashing and
    inner border

BINDING
¾ yard

BACKING
4¾ yards - vertical seam(s)
  or 2½ yards of 108" wide

OTHER
Clearly Perfect Slotted Trimmers
  A & B

***Note**: The usable width of the print strips should be at least 43".

SAMPLE QUILT
Sew Fine Batiks by Kathy Engle
  for Island Batik

QUILTING PATTERN
Champange Bubbles

PATTERN
P. 84

Radiant Reindeer Wall Hanging

PROJECT SIZE
20" x 39¼"

REINDEER SIZE
6¾" x 6¾" finished

PROJECT SUPPLIES
¼ yard white fabric
1 yard brown fabric
¾ yard print fabric
2 Rainbow Classic 9" x 12"
  Felt Squares - Black
¼ yard Heat n Bond Lite*
1 package of Missouri Star
Quilter's Best Blend Crib Batting
(3) 2" x 40" fusible fleece strips
⅝" x 24" dowel
Basting spray - recommended
6 yards medium weight red yarn
  for Rudolph's nose - optional*
Missouri Star Circle Magic Large
  5" Circle Template - optional

A scrap of red fabric can be substituted for the yarn on Rudolph's nose.

SAMPLE PROJECT
Hay... It's Christmas - Red Plaid
  by Russell Cobane for Northcott,
Kona Cotton Chocolate and White
  by Robert Kaufman Fabrics

PATTERN
P. 92

Construction Basics

General Quilting

- All seams are ¼" inch unless directions specify differently.
- Cutting instructions are given at the point when cutting is required.
- Precuts are not prewashed, therefore do not prewash other fabrics in the project.
- All strips are cut width of fabric.
- Remove all selvages.

Press Seams

- Use a steam iron on the cotton setting.
- Press the seam just as it was sewn right sides together. This "sets" the seam.
- With dark fabric on top, lift the dark fabric and press back.
- The seam allowance is pressed toward the dark side. Some patterns may direct otherwise for certain situations.
- Follow pressing arrows in the diagrams when indicated.
- Press toward borders. Pieced borders may need otherwise.
- Press diagonal seams open on binding to reduce bulk.

Borders

- Always measure the quilt top 3x before cutting borders.
- Start measuring about 4" in from each side and through the center vertically.
- Take the average of those 3 measurements.
- Cut 2 border strips to that size. Piece strips together if needed.
- Attach 1 to either side of the quilt.
- Position the border fabric on top as you sew. The feed dogs can act like rufflers. Having the border on top will prevent waviness and keep the quilt straight.
- Repeat this process for the top and bottom borders, measuring the width 3 times.
- Include the newly attached side borders in your measurements.
- Press toward the borders.

Binding

find a video tutorial at: www.msqc.co/006

- Use 2½" strips for binding.
- Sew strips end-to-end into 1 long strip with diagonal seams, aka the plus sign method (next). Press the seams open.
- Fold in half lengthwise, wrong sides together, and press.
- The entire length should equal the outside dimension of the quilt plus 15" - 20."

Plus Sign Method

find a video tutorial at: www.msqc.co/001

- Lay 1 strip across the other as if to make a plus sign, right sides together.
- Sew from top inside to bottom outside corners crossing the intersections of fabric as you sew.
- Trim excess to ¼" seam allowance.
- Press seam open.

Attach Binding

- Match raw edges of folded binding to the quilt top edge.
- Leave a 10" tail at the beginning.
- Use a ¼" seam allowance.
- Start in the middle of a long straight side.

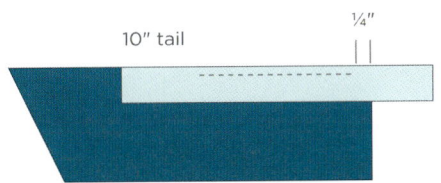

Miter Corners

- Stop sewing ¼" before the corner.
- Move the quilt out from under the presser foot.
- Clip the threads.
- Flip the binding up at a 90° angle to the edge just sewn.
- Fold the binding down along the next side to be sewn, aligning raw edges.
- The fold will lie along the edge just completed.
- Begin sewing on the fold.

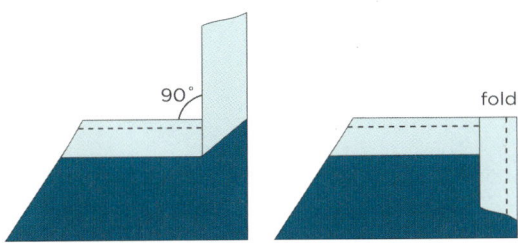

Close Binding

MSQC recommends The Binding Tool from TQM Products to finish binding perfectly every time.

- Stop sewing when you have 12" left to reach the start.
- Where the binding tails come together, trim the excess leaving only 2½" of overlap.
- It helps to pin or clip the quilt together at the 2 points where the binding starts and stops. This takes the pressure off of the binding tails while you work.
- Use the plus sign method to sew the 2 binding ends together, except this time when making the plus sign, match the edges. Using a pencil, mark your sewing line because you won't be able to see where the corners intersect. Sew across.

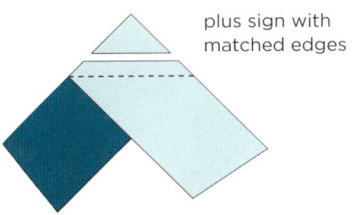

plus sign with matched edges

- Trim off the excess; press the seam open.
- Fold in half wrong sides together, and align all raw edges to the quilt top.
- Sew this last binding section to the quilt. Press.
- Turn the folded edge of the binding around to the back of the quilt and tack into place with an invisible stitch or machine stitch if you wish.